BEN HARPER AND
WHITE LIES FOR D...

MW00800566

Music transcriptions by Pete Billmann and David Stocker

ISBN 978-1-4234-7934-5

7777 W. BLUEMOUND RD. P.O. BOX 13819 MILWAUKEE, WI 53213

In Australia Contact:
Hal Leonard Australia Pty. Ltd.
4 Lentara Court
Cheltenham, Victoria, 3192 Australia
Email: ausadmin@halleonard.com.au

Visit Hal Leonard Online at
www.halleonard.com

Number With No Name

Words and Music by Ben Harper, Jason Mozersky, Jordan Richardson and Jesse Ingalls

Gtr. 1: Open D tuning, Capo IV:
(low to high) D-A-D-F♯-A-D

Intro
Moderately ♩ = 85

F♯7
**(D7)

*Gtr. 1 (slight dist.)

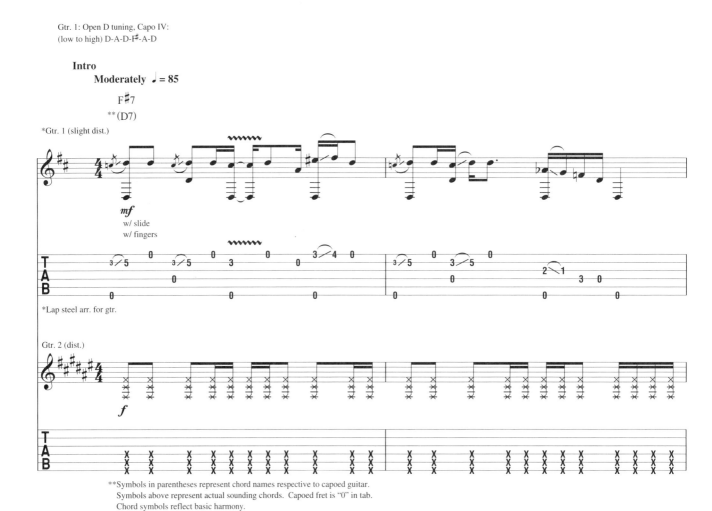

mf
w/ slide
w/ fingers

*Lap steel arr. for gtr.

Gtr. 2 (dist.)

f

**Symbols in parentheses represent chord names respective to capoed guitar.
Symbols above represent actual sounding chords. Capoed fret is "0" in tab.
Chord symbols reflect basic harmony.

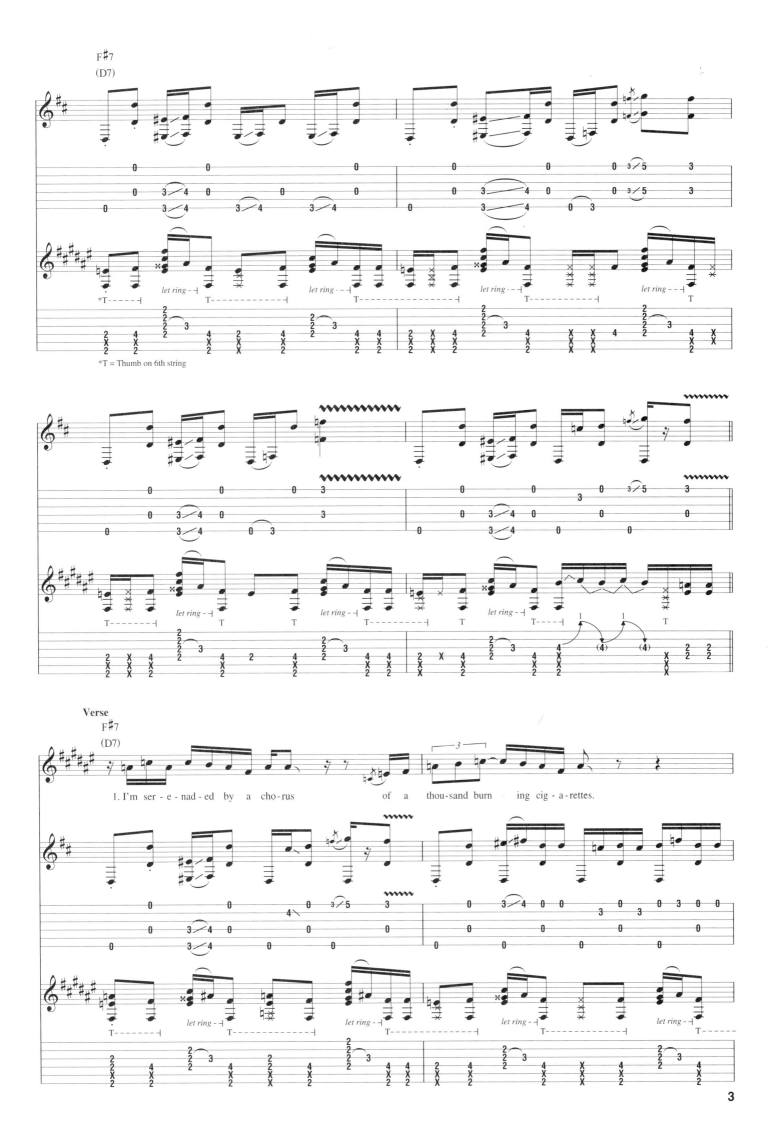

*T = Thumb on 6th string

1. I'm ser-e-nad-ed by a cho-rus of a thou-sand burn-ing cig-a-rettes.

You've been tak - in' chanc - es, ma-ma, while I've been _ plac - in' bets.

A7
(F7)

So, tell _ it to the ash - es, _____ they'd know we _ served. _

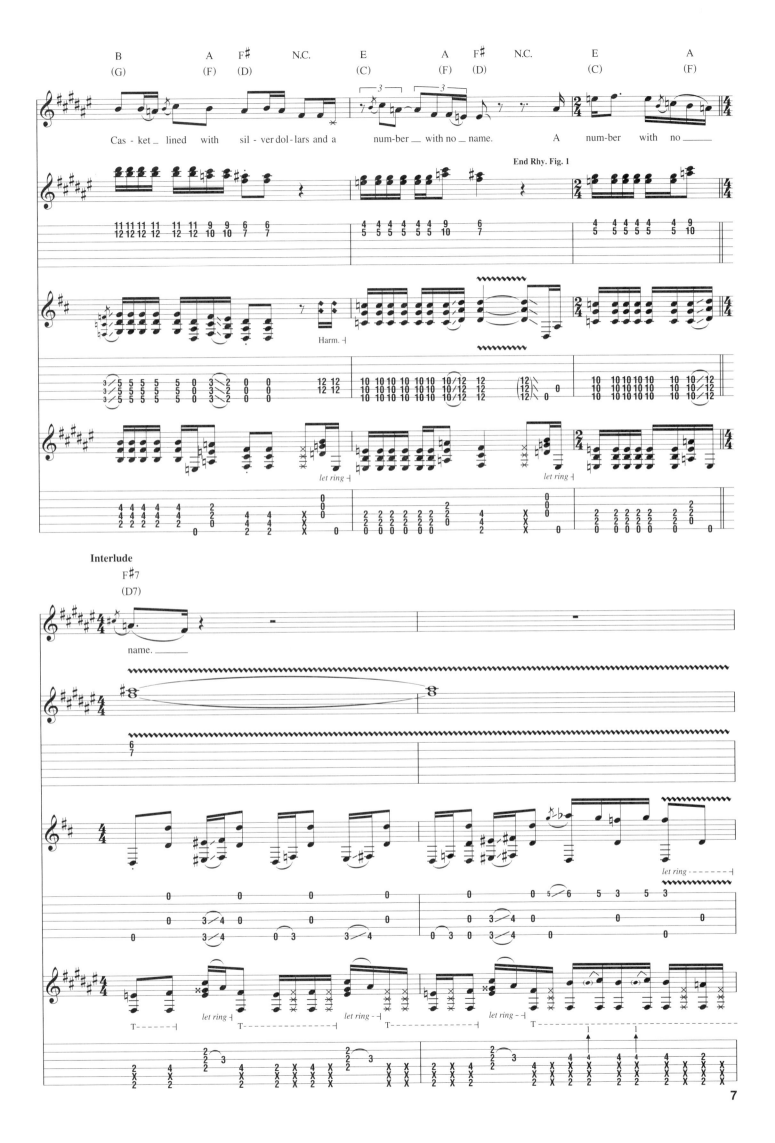

A7
(F7)

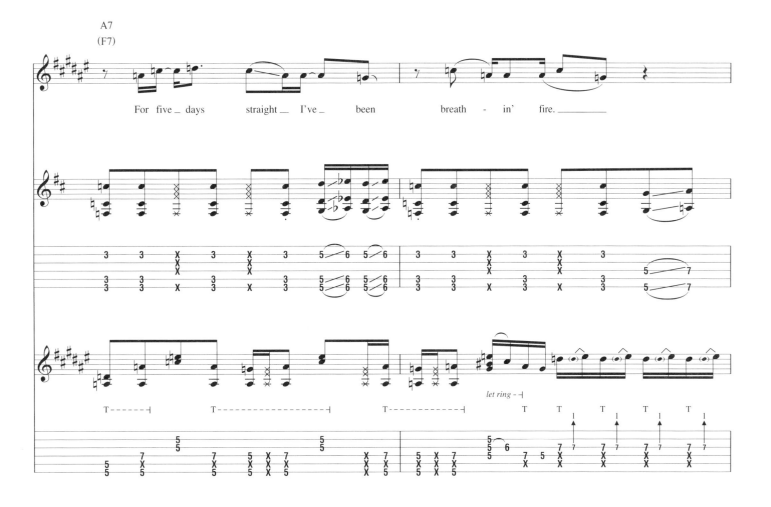

For five days straight I've been breath - in' fire.

F#7
(D7)

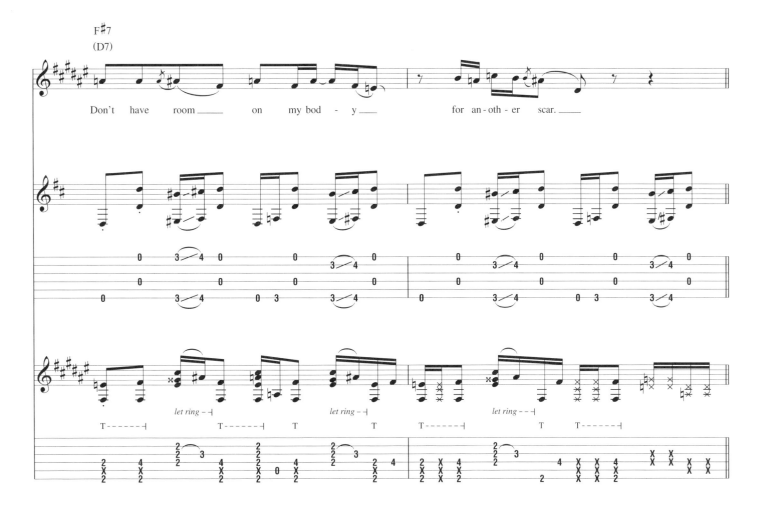

Don't have room on my bod - y for an - oth - er scar.

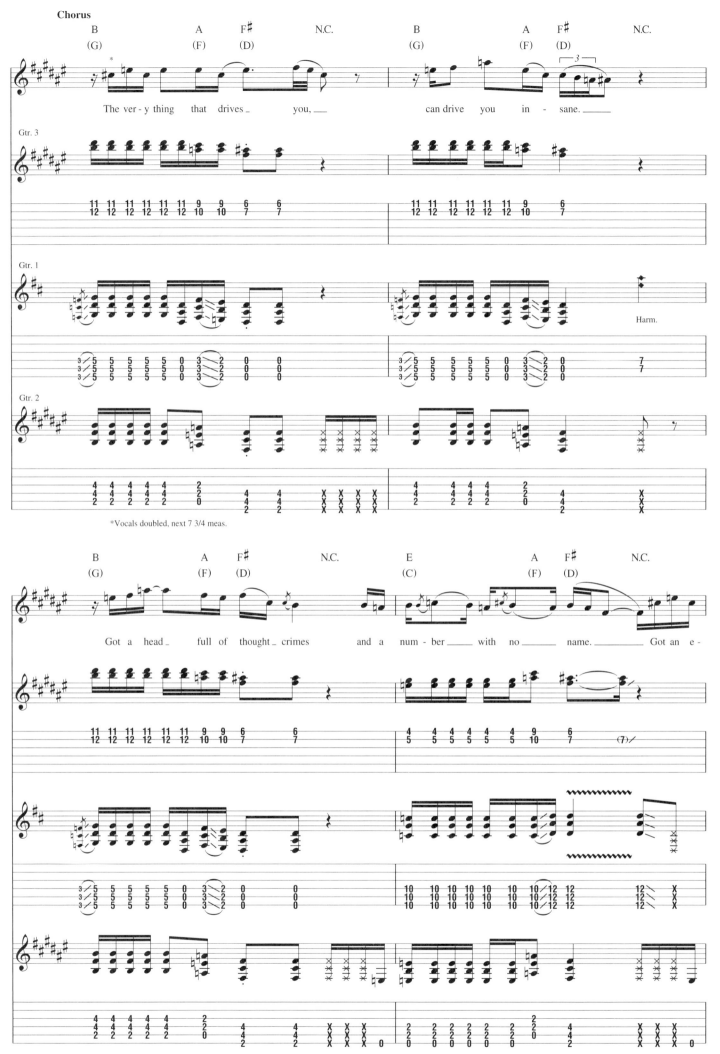

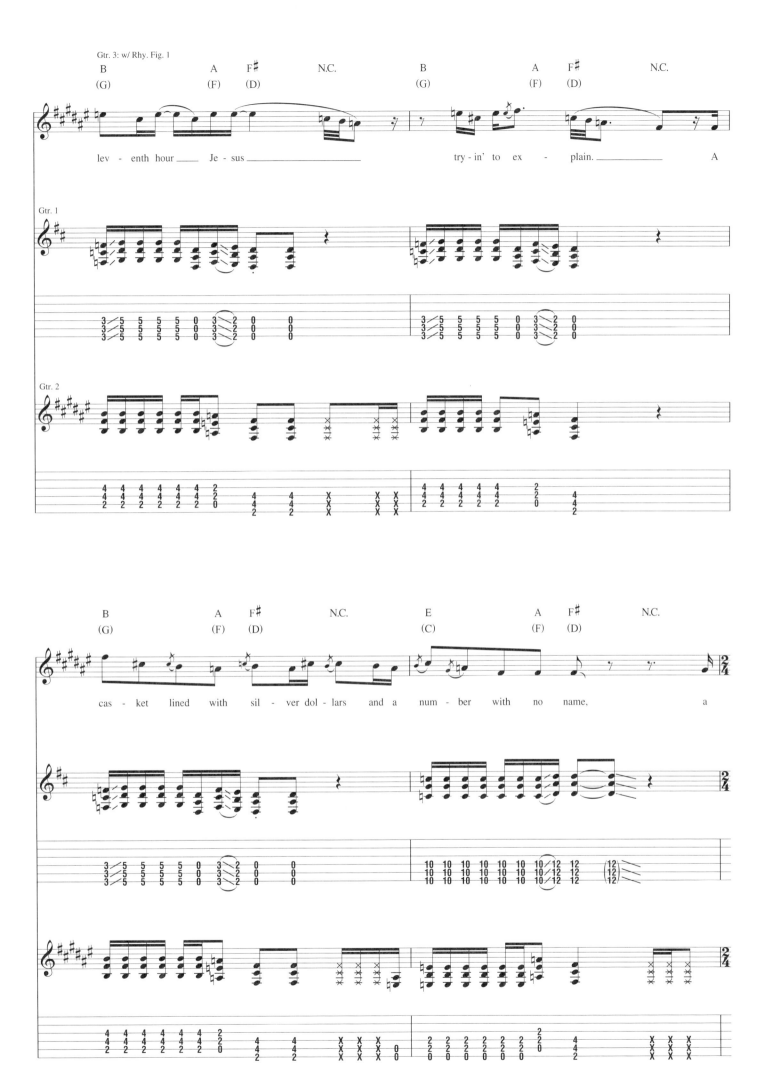

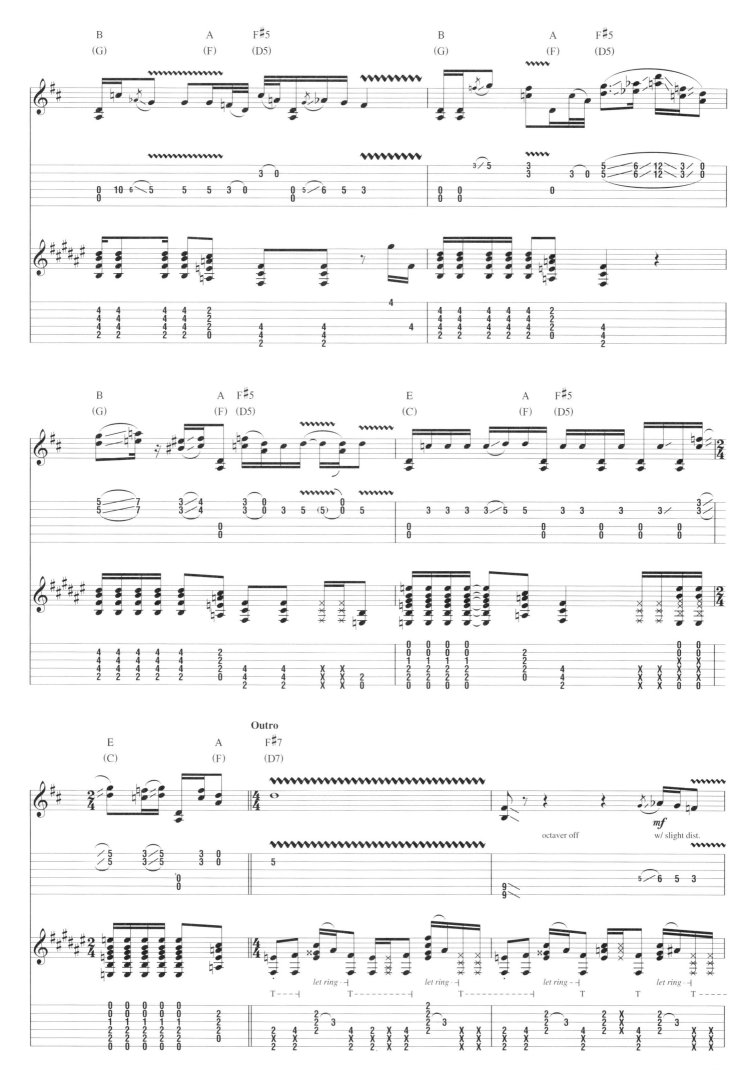

Up to You Now

Words and Music by Ben Harper, Jason Mozersky, Jordan Richardson and Jesse Ingalls

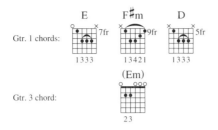

Gtr. 1 chords:

Gtr. 3 chord:

Gtr. 3: Capo II

Intro
Moderately fast ♩ = 120

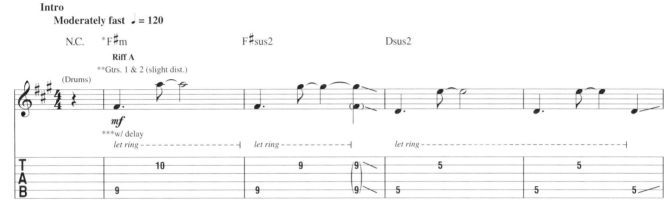

*Chord symbols reflect implied harmony.

**Composite arrangement

***Set for dotted eighth-note regeneration w/ 2 repeats. Gtr. 1 only.

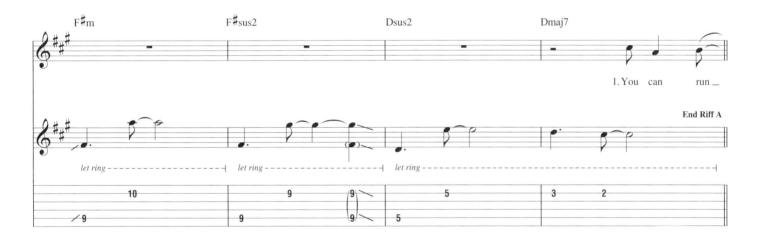

Verse

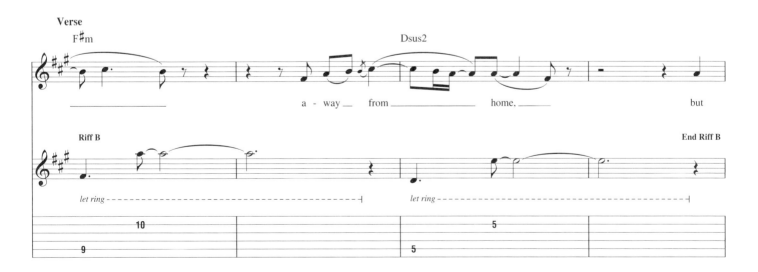

you can't _____ run a - way _____ from your pain. Now,

I sit _____ here ___ a - lone. _____ There's al -

ways _____ some - one ___ else _____ to blame. ___

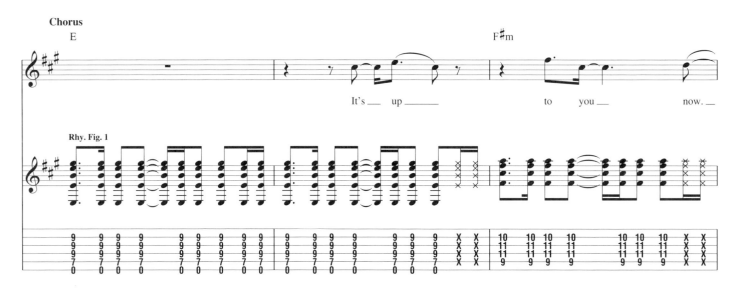

It's ___ up _____ to you ___ now.

17

Interlude

Verse

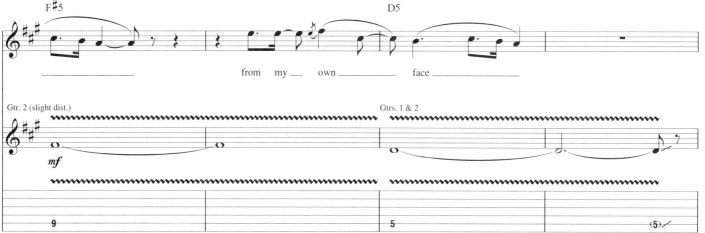

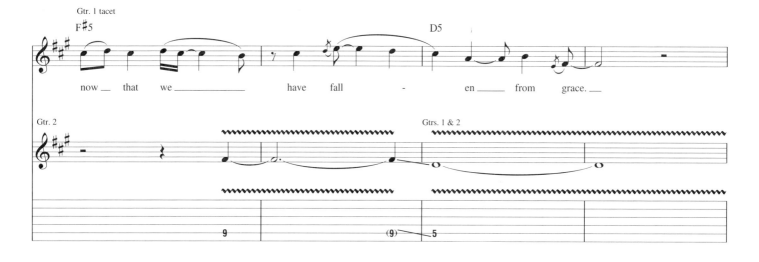

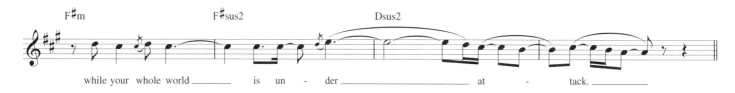

18

Chorus

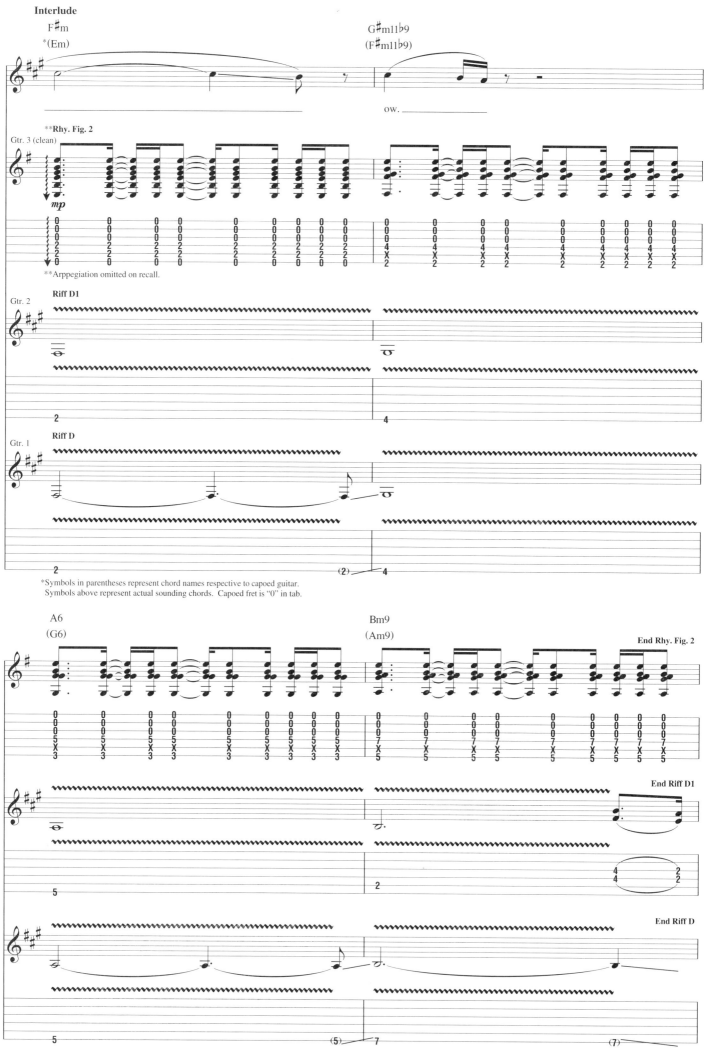

Interlude

F#m
*(Em)

G#m11b9
(F#m11b9)

ow.

**Rhy. Fig. 2
Gtr. 3 (clean)

mp

**Arppegiation omitted on recall.

Gtr. 2   Riff D1

Gtr. 1   Riff D

*Symbols in parentheses represent chord names respective to capoed guitar.
Symbols above represent actual sounding chords. Capoed fret is "0" in tab.

A6
(G6)

Bm9
(Am9)

End Rhy. Fig. 2

End Riff D1

End Riff D

Oh, ___ there's ___ no ___

Bridge

Gtrs. 1 & 3 tacet

sound ___ loud-er ___ than war. ___ And we don't

have ___ to-mor-row ___ an-y-more. You wrote a

Gtr. 2

let ring

Gtr. 1

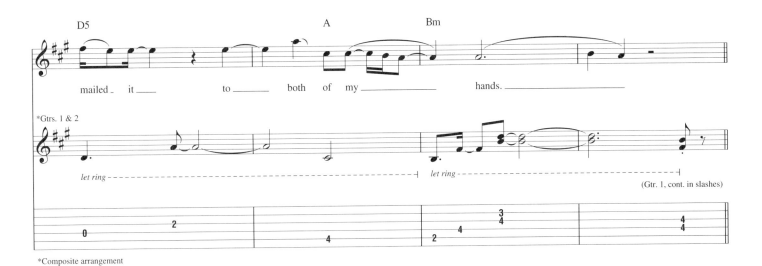

*Composite arrangement

So it's up,

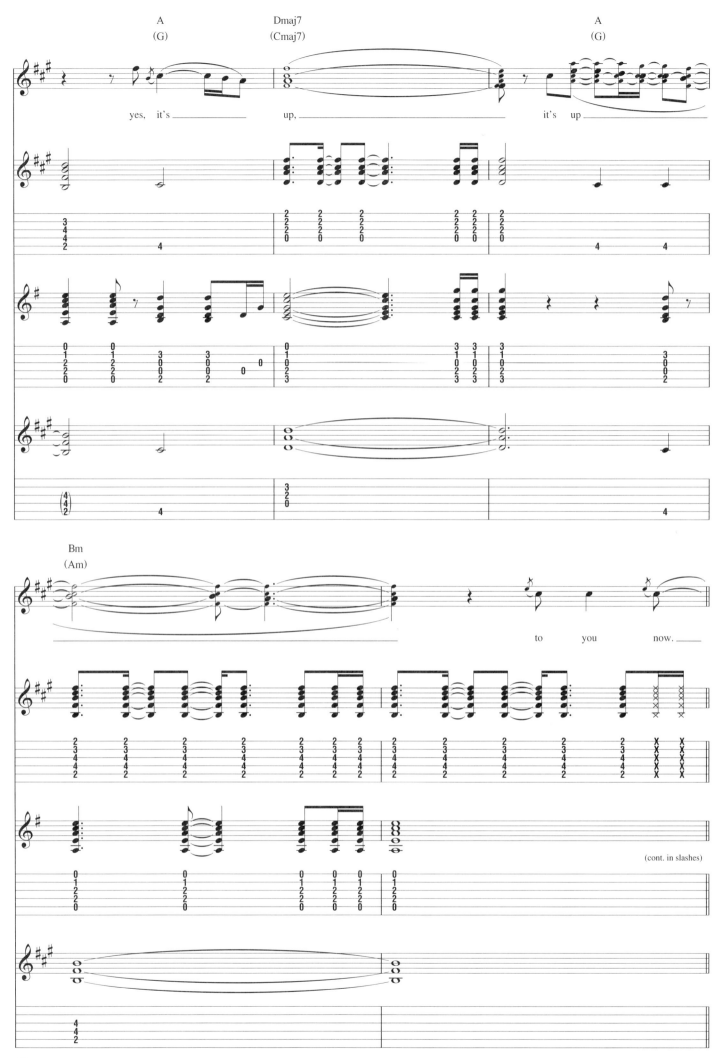

Outro

(Em)

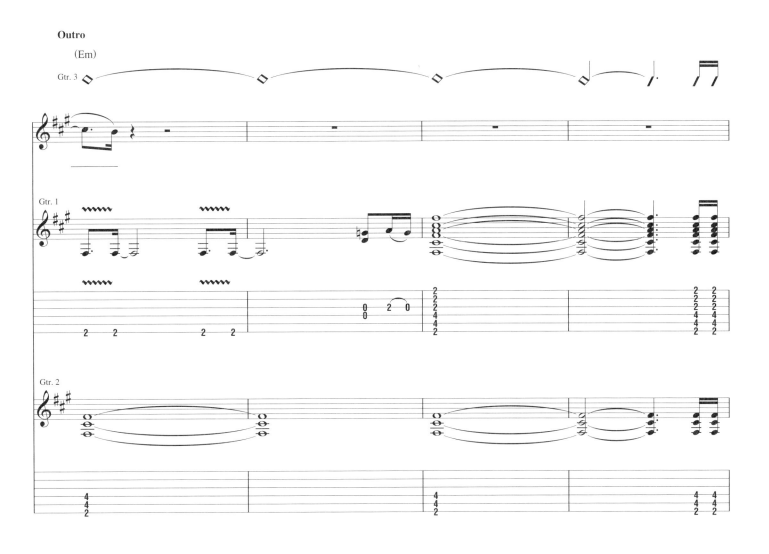

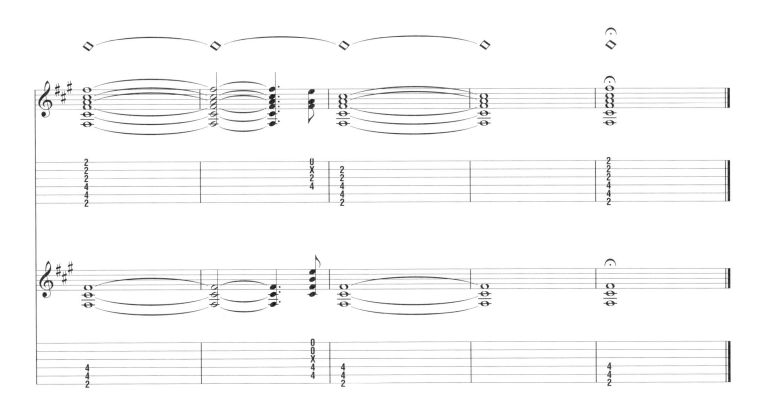

Shimmer and Shine

Words and Music by Ben Harper

*Symbols in parentheses represent chord names respective to capoed guitars.
Symbols above represent actual sounding chords. Capoed fret is "0" in tab.
Chord symbols reflect overall harmony.

**Lap steel arr. for gtr.

***Slide positioned halfway between the 8th & 9th frets.

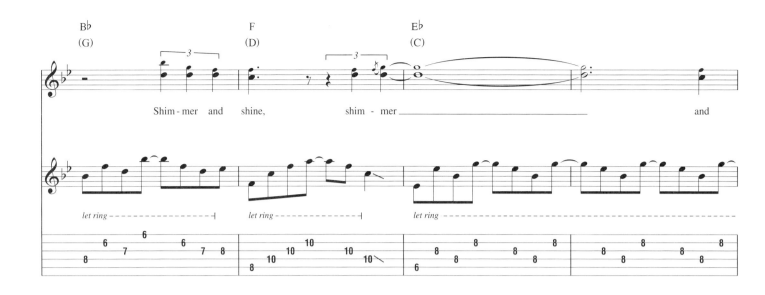

Shim - mer and shine, shim - mer _____ and

Guitar Solo

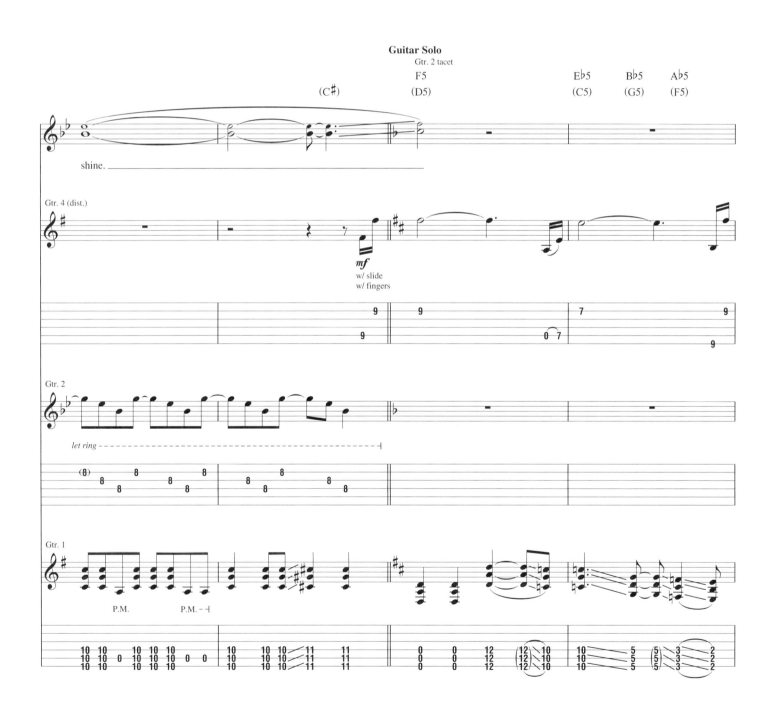

shine. _____

Lay There and Hate Me

Words and Music by Ben Harper, Jason Mozersky, Jordan Richardson and Jesse Ingalls

Gtr. 1: Drop D tuning:
(low to high) D-A-D-G-B-E

Gtr. 5: Open D tuning:
(low to high) D-A-D-F#-A-D

*Wurlitzer elec. pno. arr. for gtr.

**Chord symbols reflect implied harmony.

One side to the oth - er, you toss ___ and turn. ___

End Riff A

Gtr. 1: w/ Riff A (2 times)

*C

G

Nev - er trust a wom - an, nev - er trust a wom - an who loves the blues. _

Gtr. 2

let ring - - - - -⌐ let ring - - - - -⌐ let ring - - - - -⌐ let ring - - - - -⌐

*Chord symbols reflect overall harmony.

Bkgd. Voc.: w/ Voc. Fig. 1

Dm7

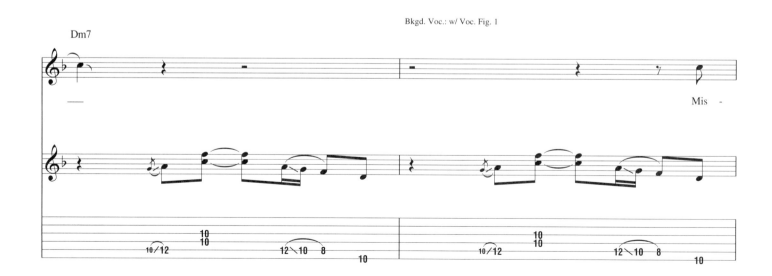

___ Mis -

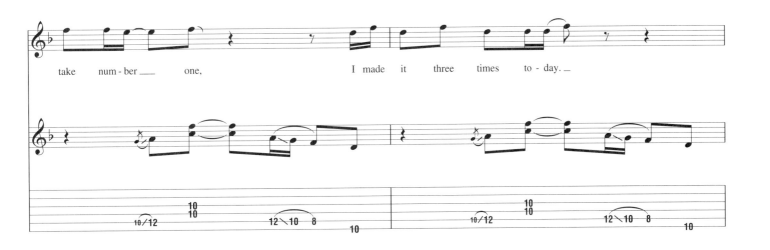

take num-ber ___ one, I made it three times to-day. ___

Bkgd. Voc.: w/ Voc. Fig. 1

We best talk o - ver how ___ there's noth - in' left ___ to say. _____ I

feel ___ like ___ an un - der - paid _____ con - cu - bine ___ who's o - ver - stayed ___ her wel-

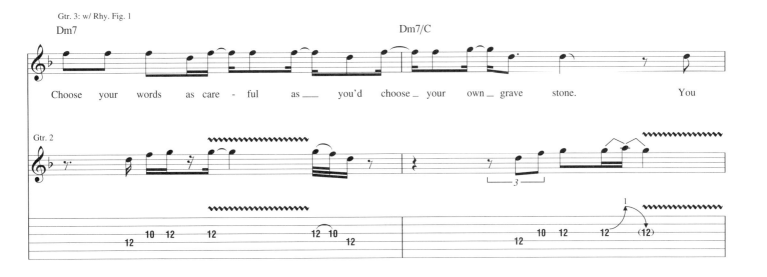

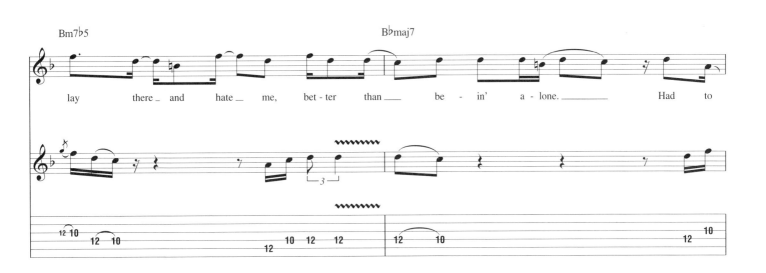

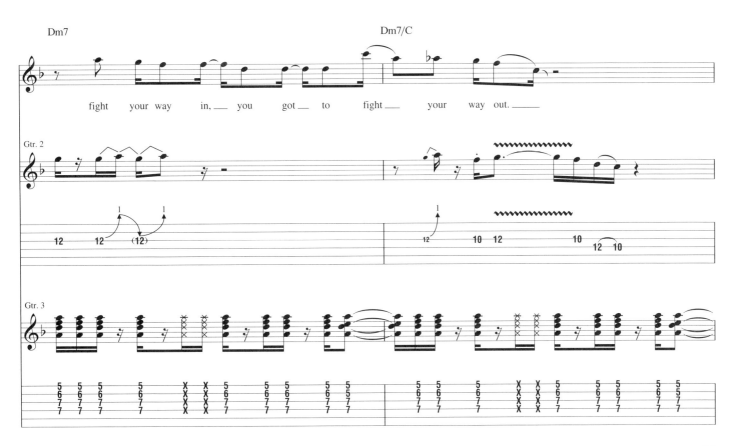

Chorus

Gtr. 3: w/ Rhy. Fig. 1 (2 1/2 times)

Gtrs. 1 & 2 tacet

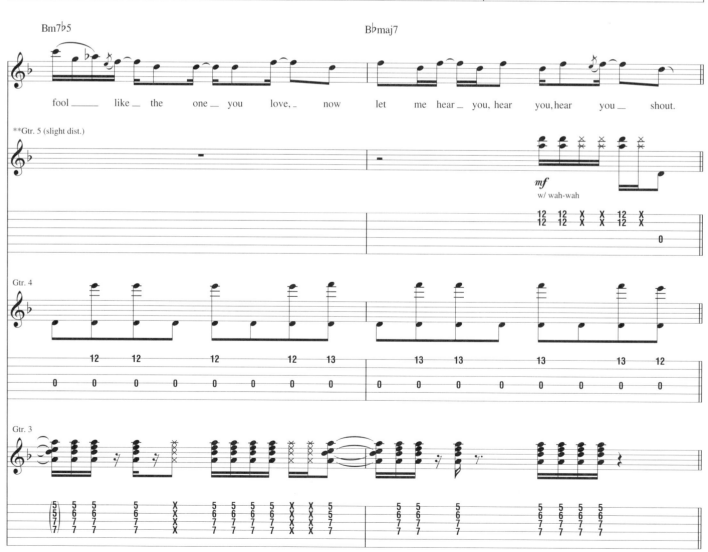

sit-tin' a - lone. _____ Nev - er trust a wom - an who loves _____

_____ the blues. _____

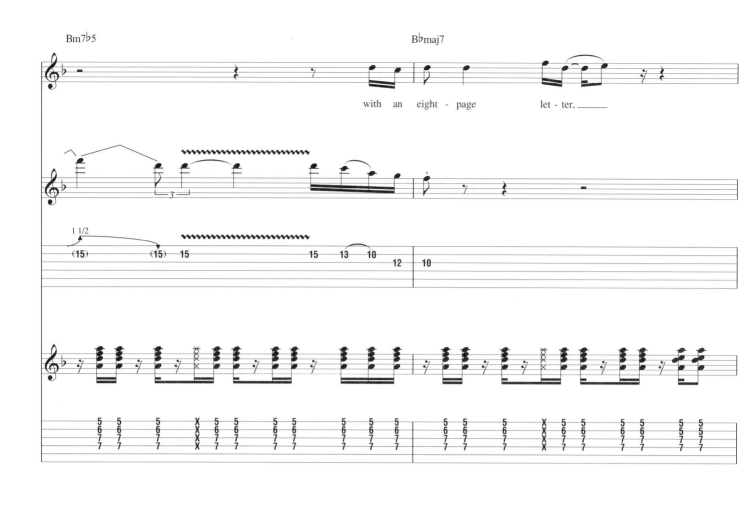

with an eight - page letter, _____

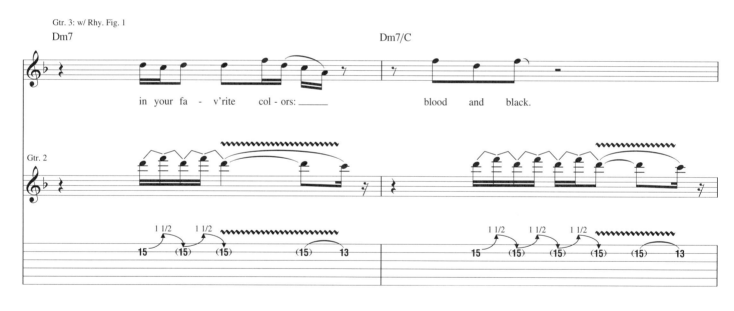

Gtr. 3: w/ Rhy. Fig. 1

in your fa - v'rite col - ors: _____ blood and black.

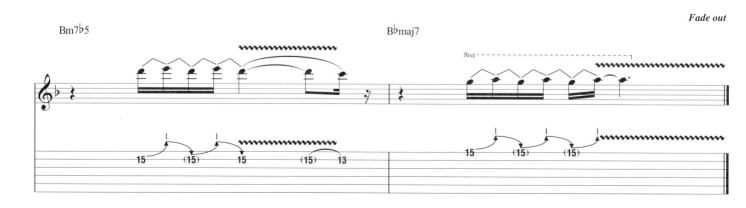

Fade out

Why Must You Always Dress in Black

Words and Music by Ben Harper, Jason Mozersky, Jordan Richardson and Jesse Ingalls

Gtr. 2: Open Em tuning:
(low to high) E-B-E-G-B-E

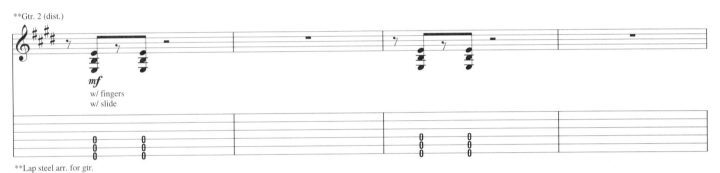

mor-row's shin - in' off ___ our face, ___ yes - ter-day's ___ shad - ow _ is at ___ our back, _

at our back. ___

So, ___

why must you al - ways dress in black? _____

Verse

Gtr. 1: w/ Riff A (6 times)

2. Peo-ple, they don't take ad - vice, they on - ly give

Gtr. 2

let ring - - - - - - - - - - - - - - -

_____ it.

And the on -

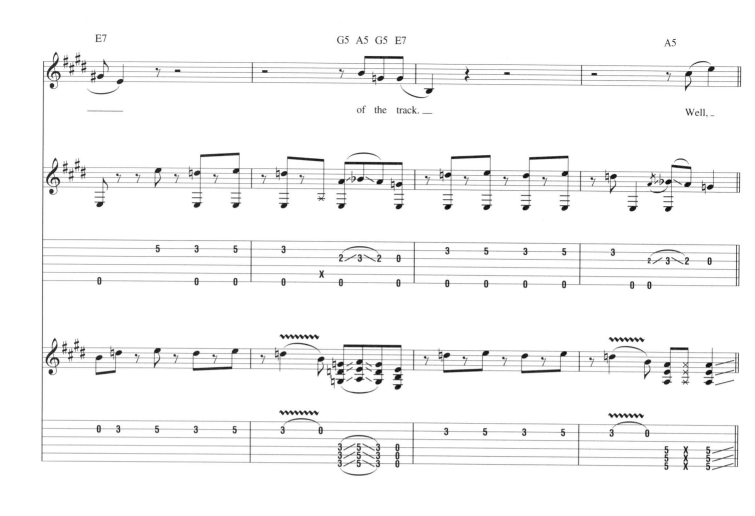

of the track. __   Well, _

Chorus

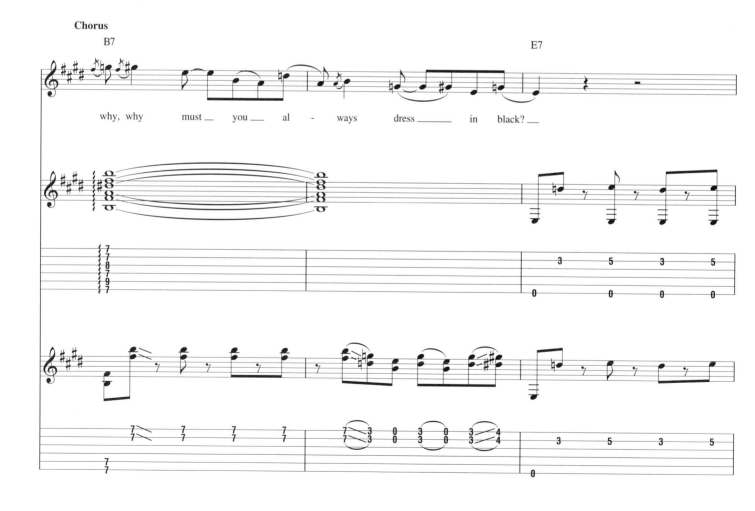

why, why must __ you __ al - ways dress _____ in black? __

woke _____ up slow, feel-ing like _ a shell _____ of _ a man.

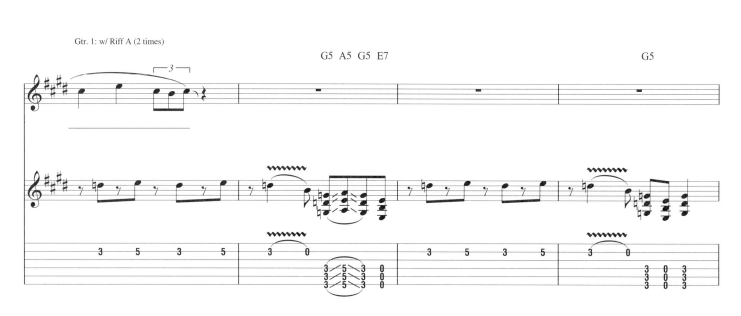

Gtr. 1: w/ Riff A (2 times)

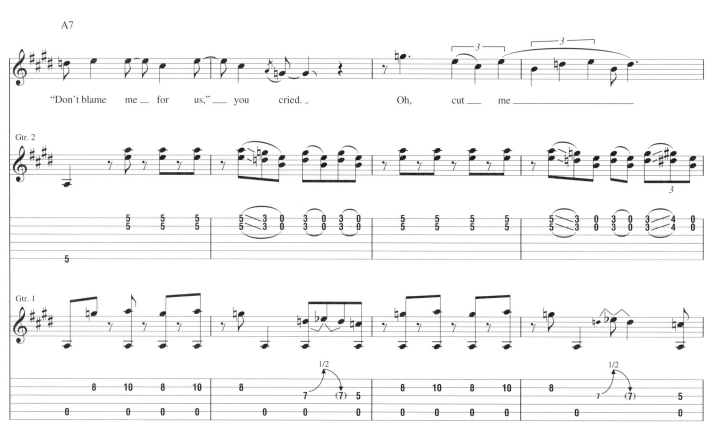

"Don't blame me _ for us," _ you cried. _ Oh, cut _ me _____

*Chord symbols reflect harmony implied by bass, next 38 meas.

4. She wore ___ high heels, _____ the ones _____ that ___ could pierce ___ your ____ heart, _____

pierce ___ your __ heart. ___ Just 'cause ___ you go down in his - t'ry _____

does-n't mean ___ you're _ real-ly all _____ that _____ smart.

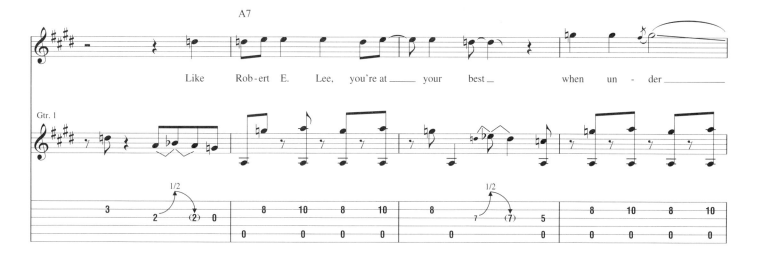

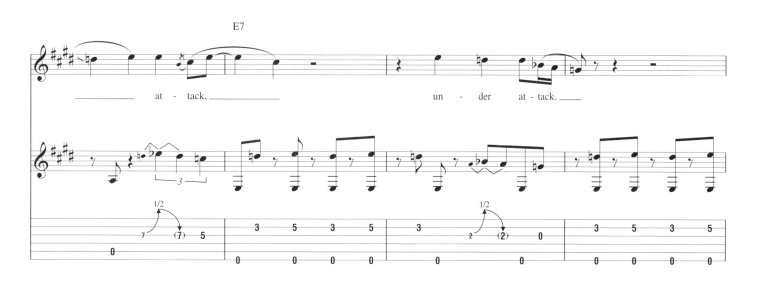

Chorus

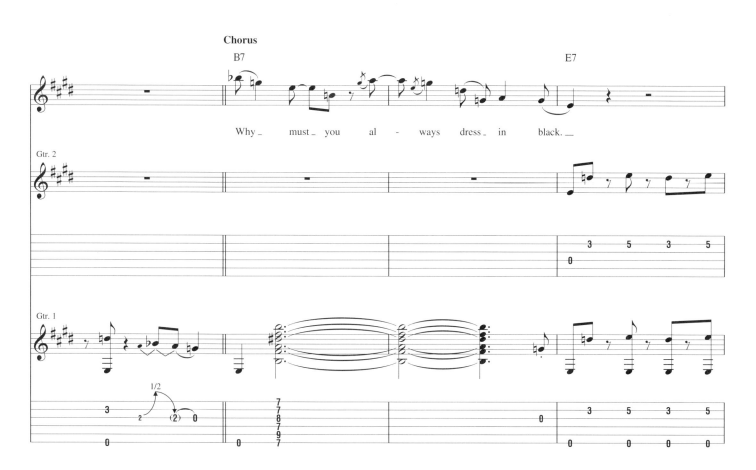

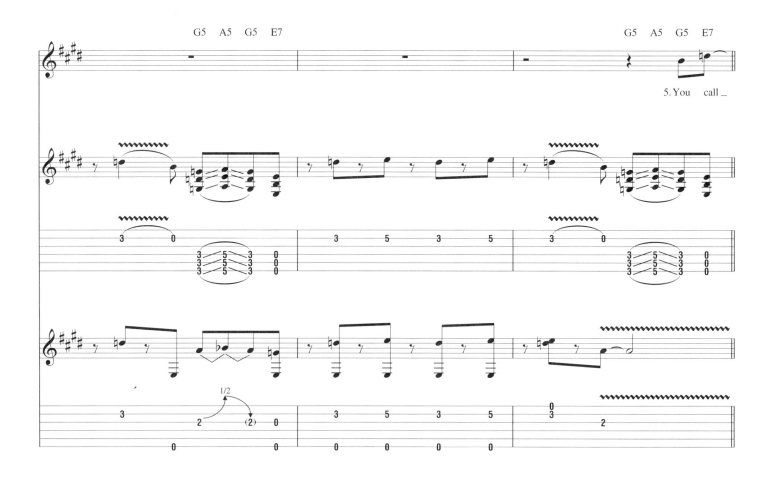

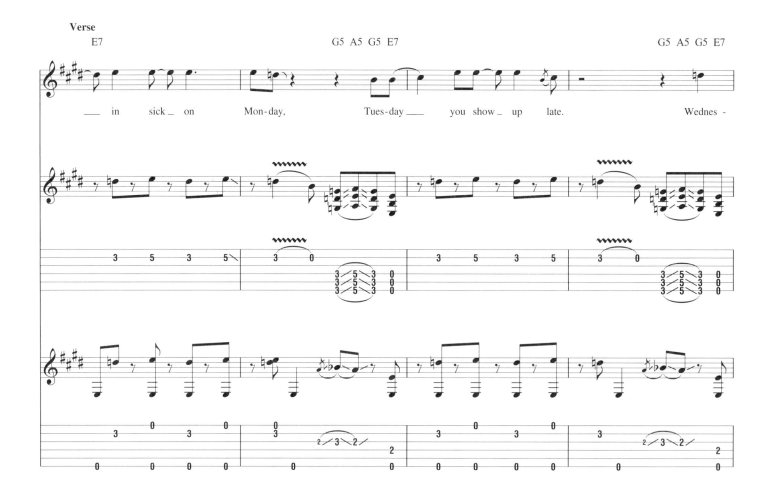

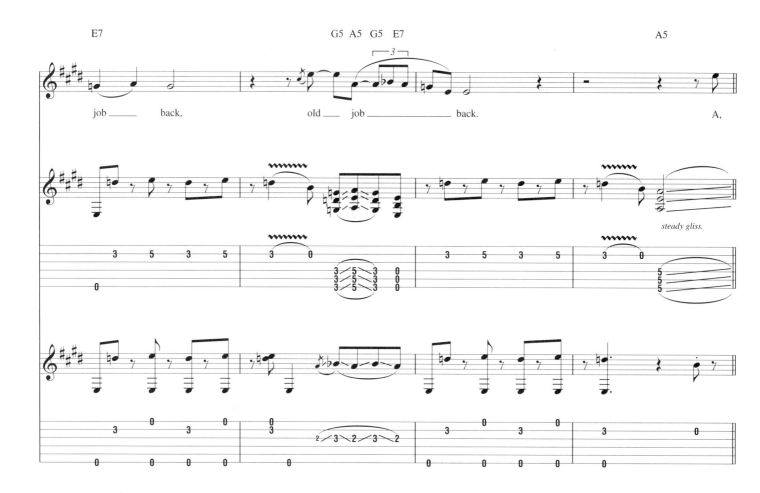

job _____ back,   old _____ job _____ back.   A,

Chorus

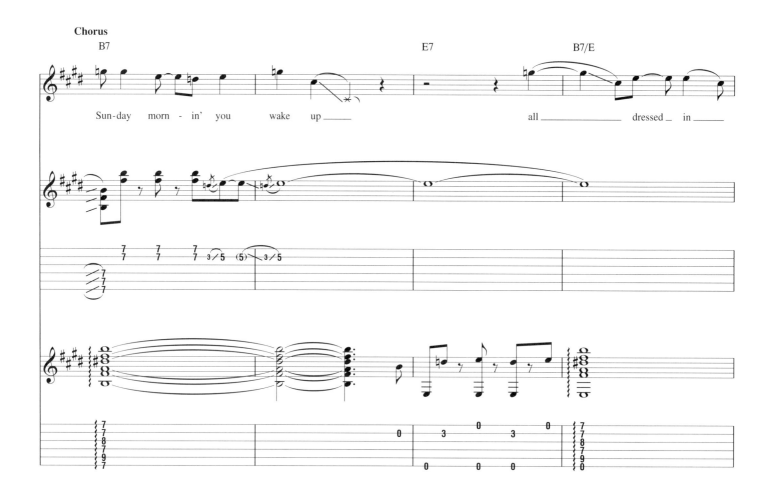

Sun-day morn - in' you wake up _____   all _____ dressed _ in _____

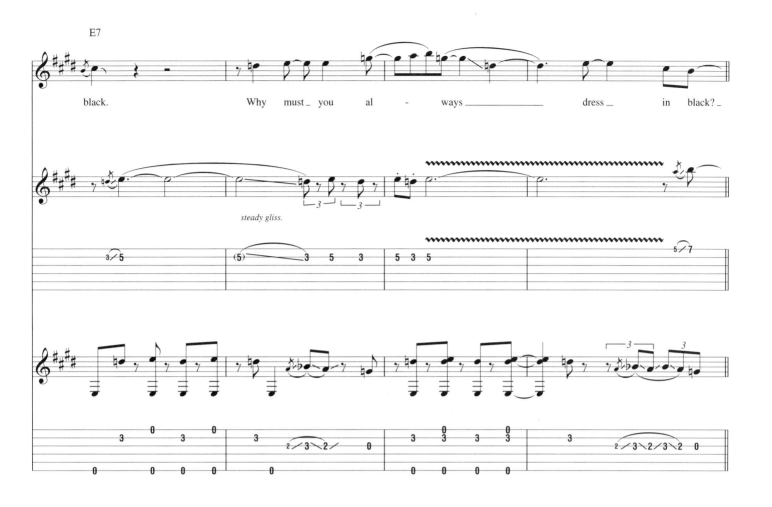

black.   Why must you al - ways   dress in black?

steady gliss.

Outro-Lap Steel Solo

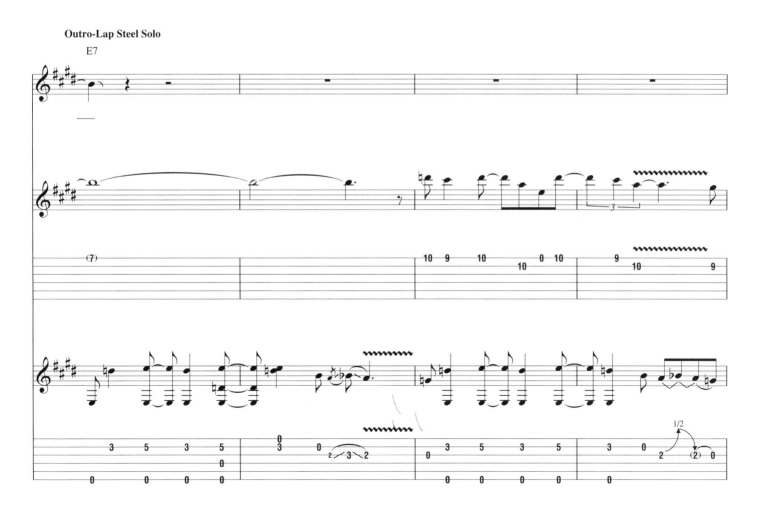

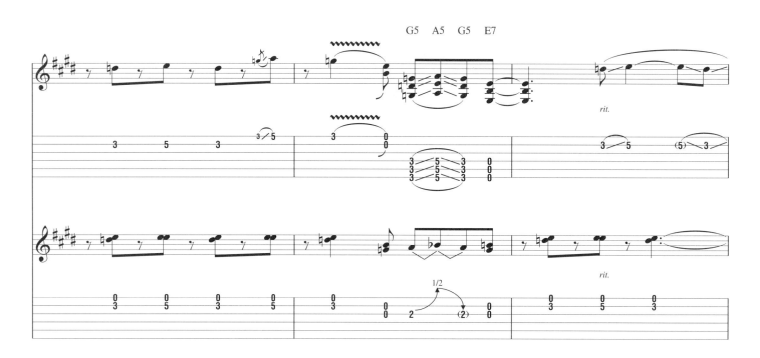

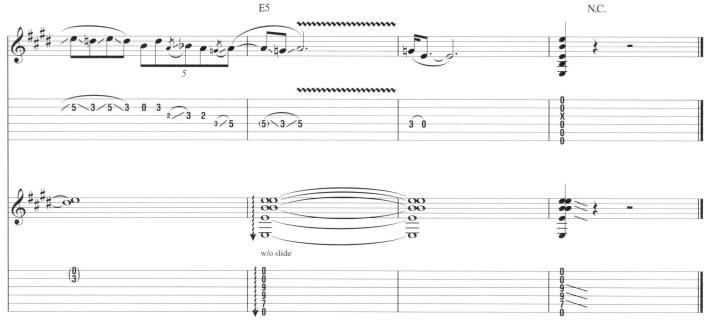

Skin Thin

Words and Music by Ben Harper, Jason Mozersky, Jordan Richardson and Jesse Ingalls

3. Now that we've grown up,

Fly One Time

Words and Music by Ben Harper, Jason Mozersky, Jordan Richardson and Jesse Ingalls

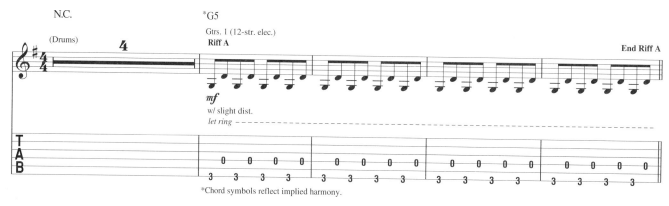

Tune down 1 step:
(low to high) D-G-C-F-A-D

Intro
Moderately ♩ = 111

*Chord symbols reflect implied harmony.

Verse

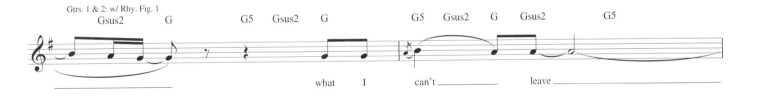

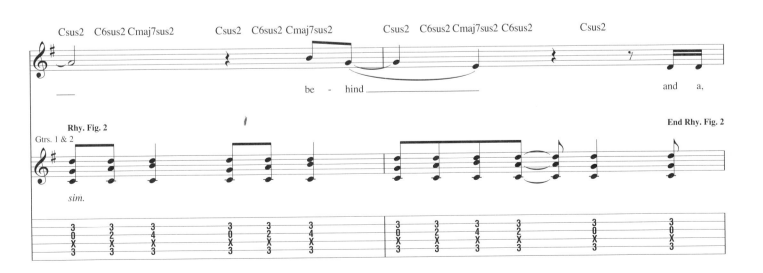

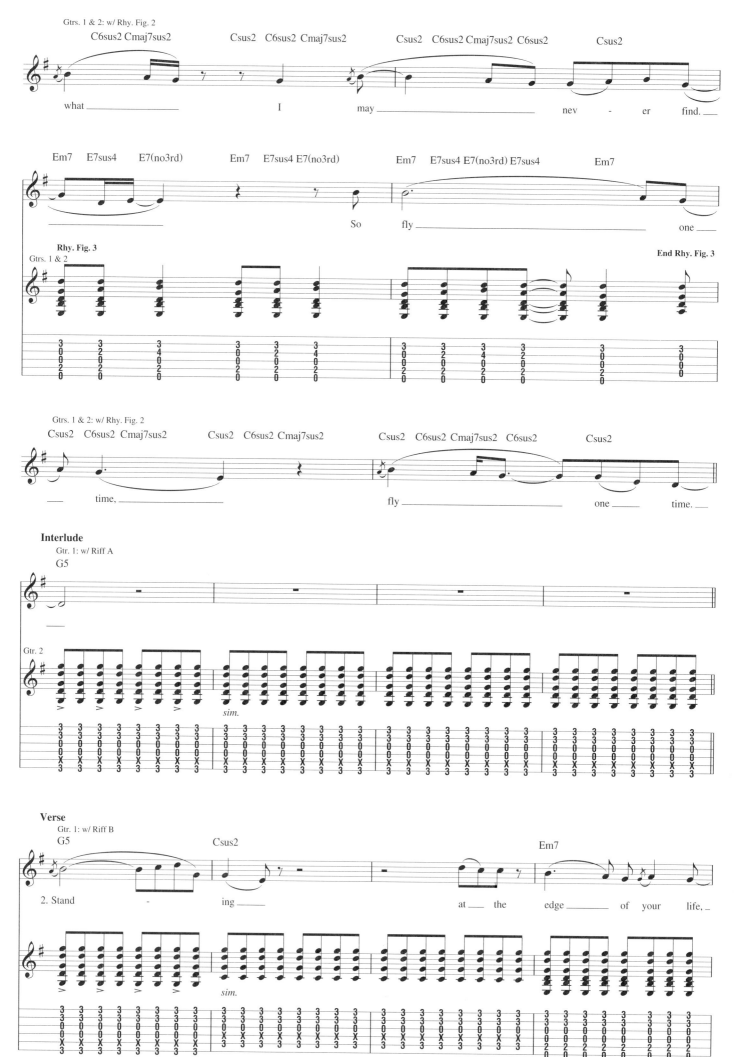

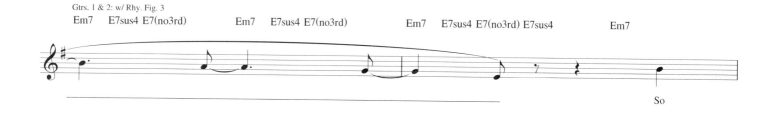

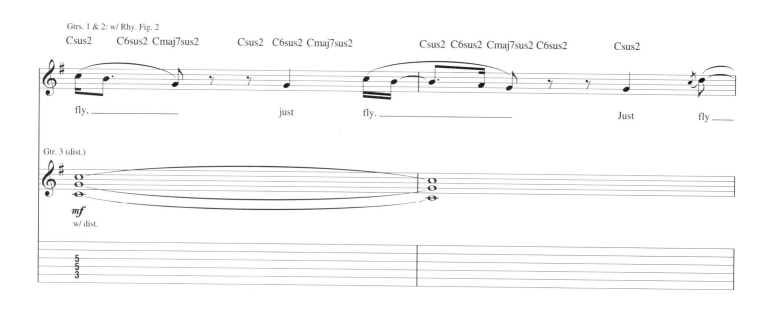

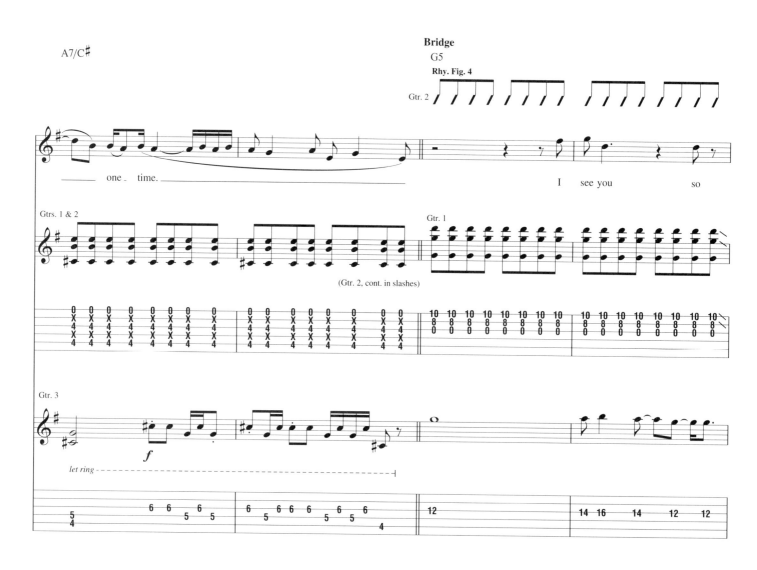

clear - ly, _____ so clear - ly, _____ up so _____

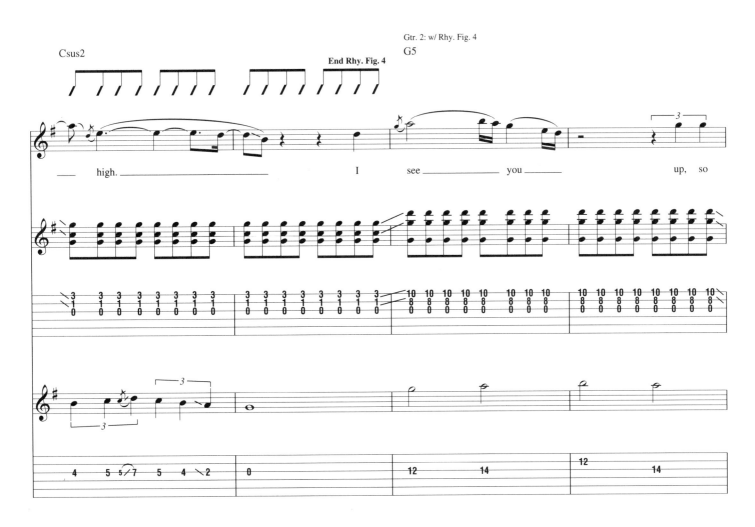

Gtr. 2: w/ Rhy. Fig. 4

End Rhy. Fig. 4

_____ high. _____ I see _____ you _____ up, so

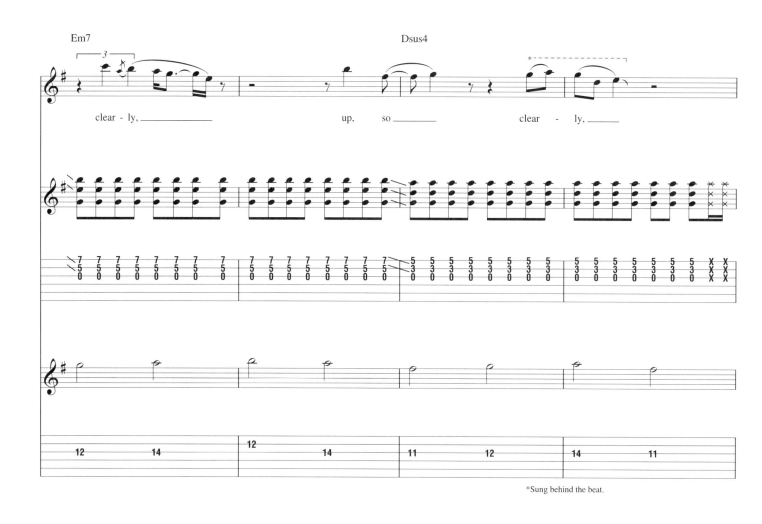

*Sung behind the beat.

Gtr. 2: w/ Rhy. Fig. 4 (last 2 meas.)

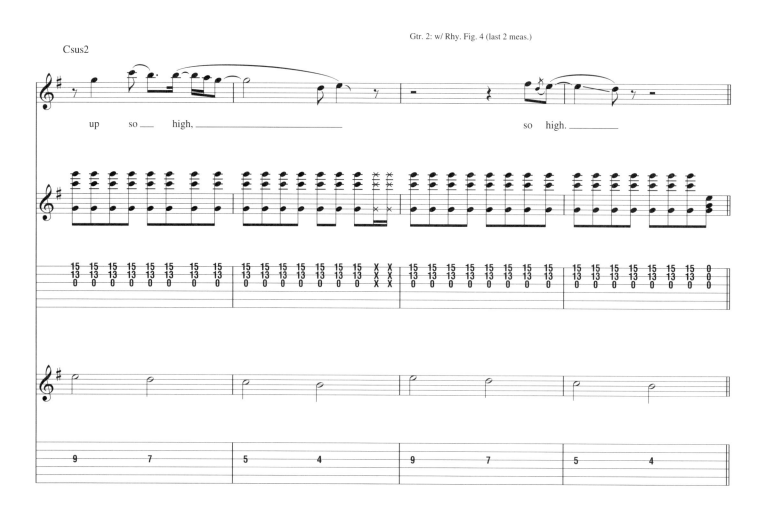

Chorus

Gtrs. 1 & 2: w/ Rhy. Fig. 1 (2 times)

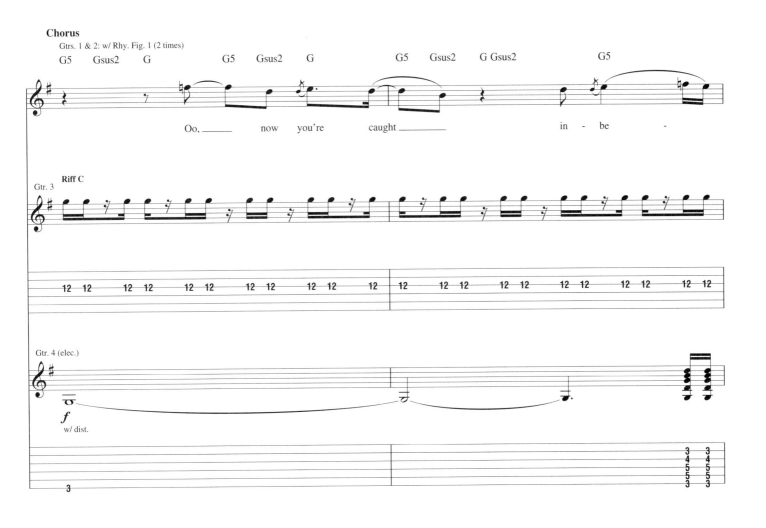

Oo,_____ now you're caught_____ in - be -

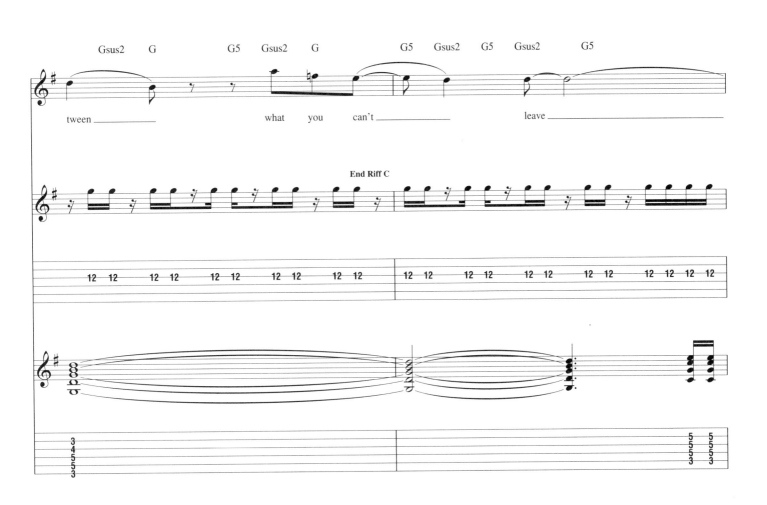

tween_____ what you can't_____ leave_____

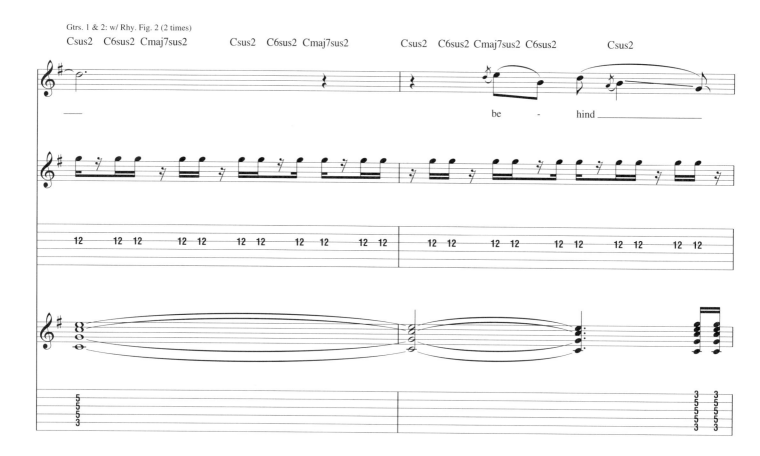

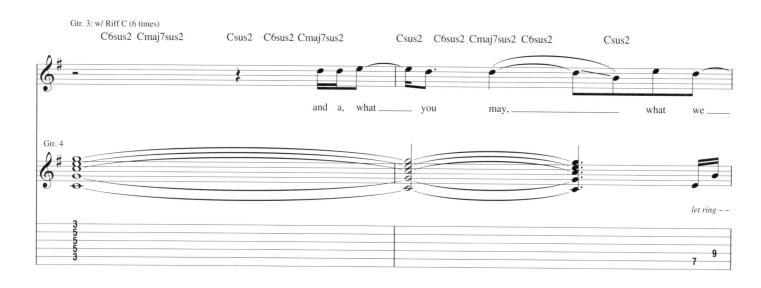

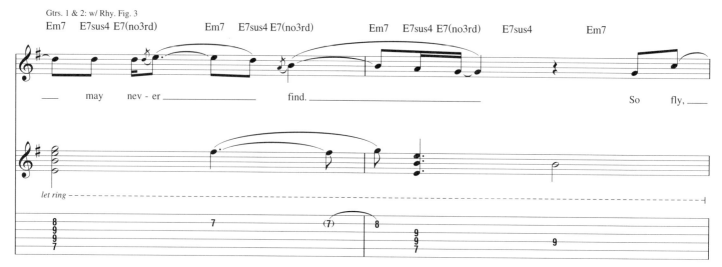

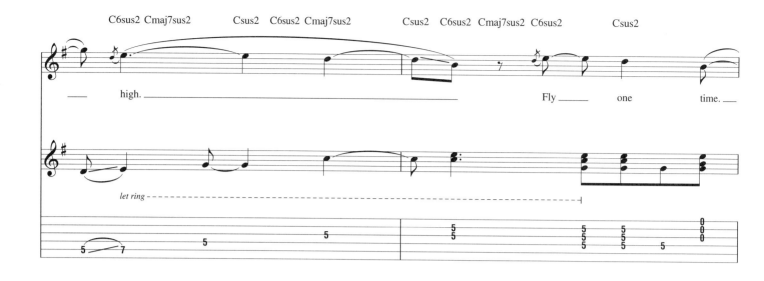

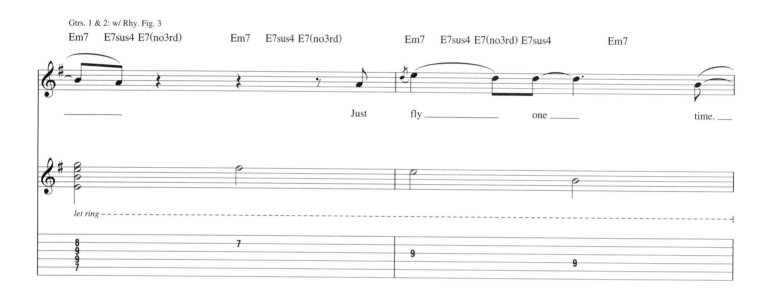

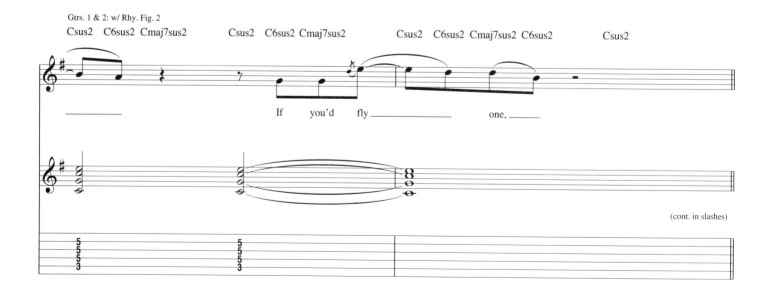

Keep It Together (So I Can Fall Apart)

Words and Music by Ben Harper, Jason Mozersky, Jordan Richardson and Jesse Ingalls

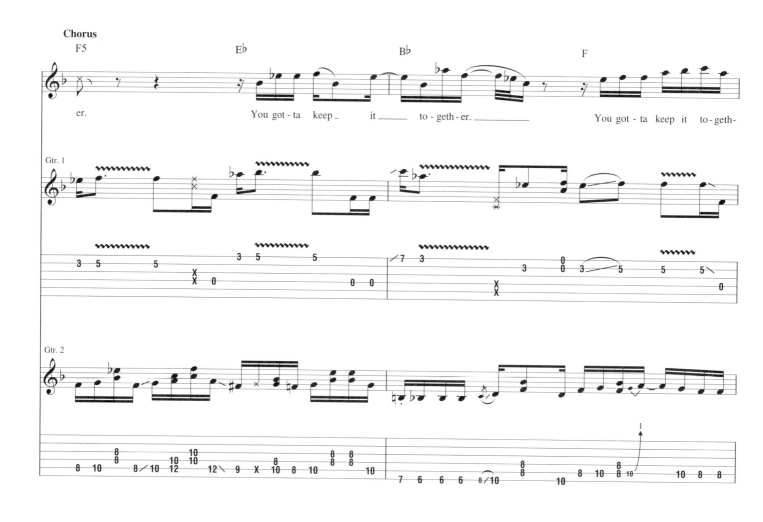

er. You got-ta keep it to-geth-er. You got-ta keep it to-geth-

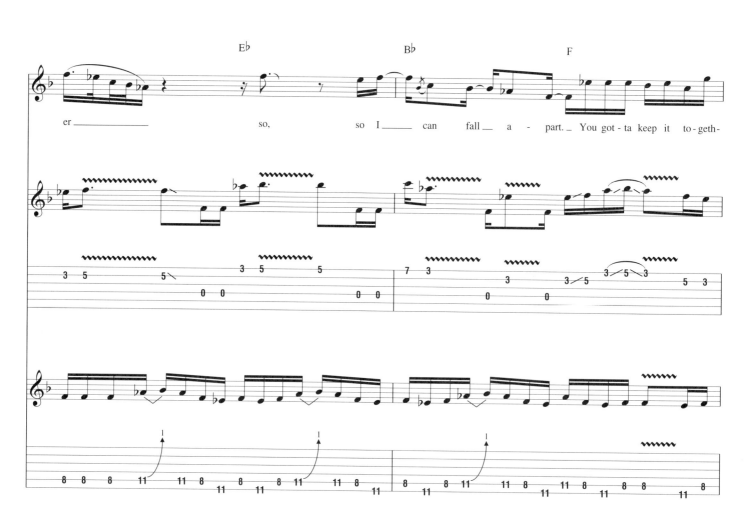

er so, so I can fall a-part. You got-ta keep it to-geth-

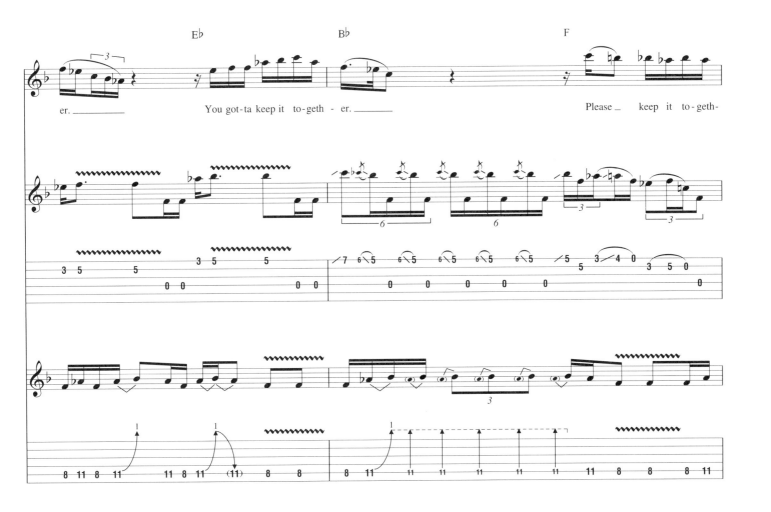

You got-ta keep it to-geth - er. _____ Please _ keep it to-geth-

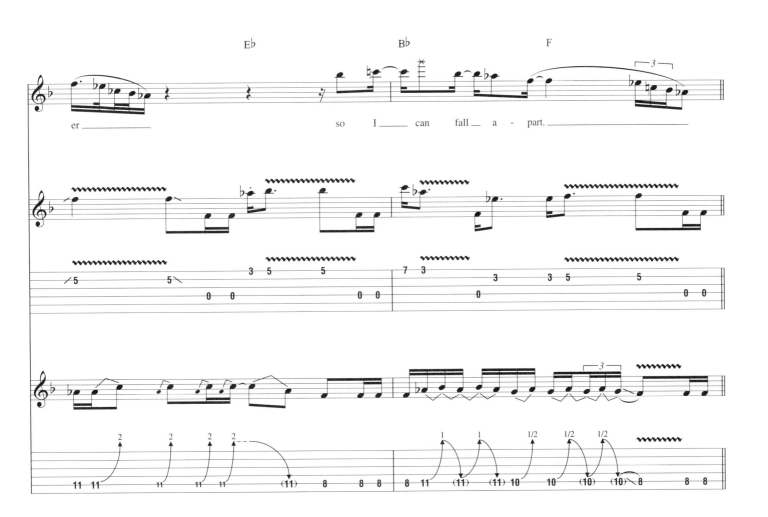

er _____ so I ___ can fall a - part. _____

93

Interlude

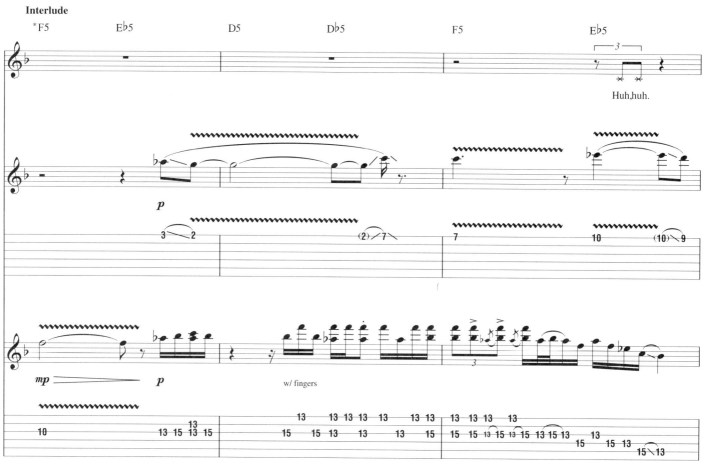

*Chord symbols reflect overall harmony.

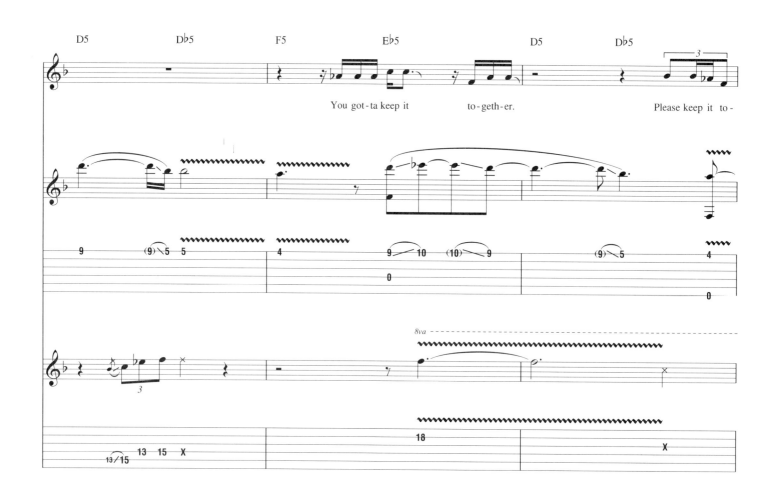

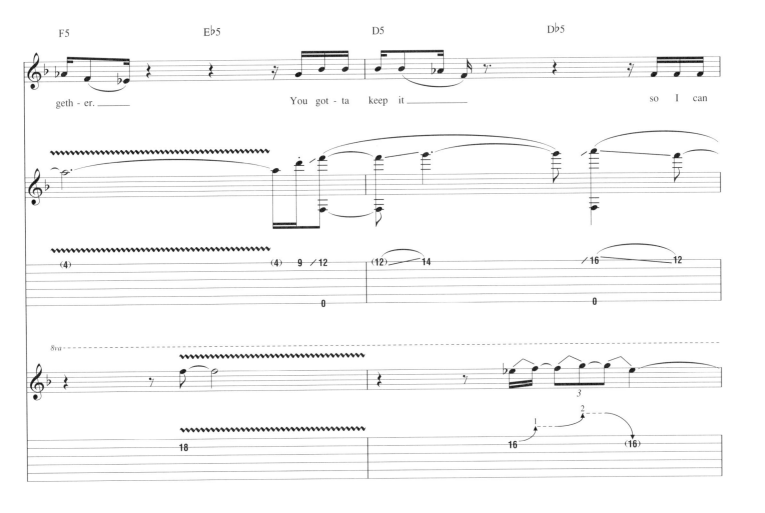

geth - er. _____ You got - ta keep it _____ so I can

fall a - part, _____ so I can fall a, fall a - part, fall _____ a - part.

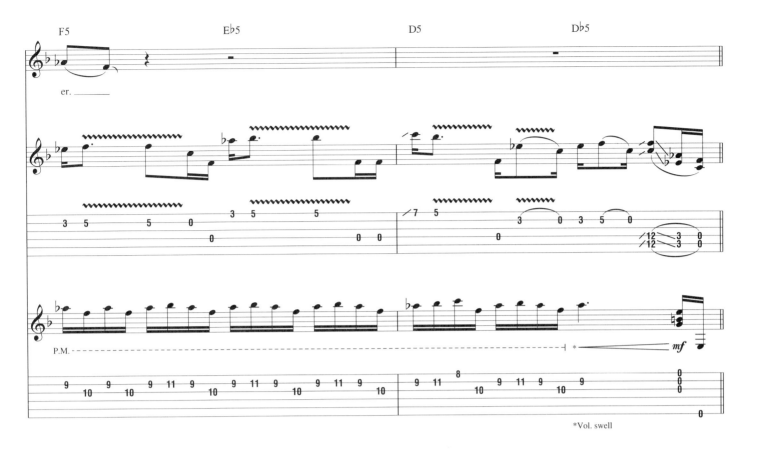

Chorus

Gtr. 1: w/ Rhy. Fig. 1 (8 times)

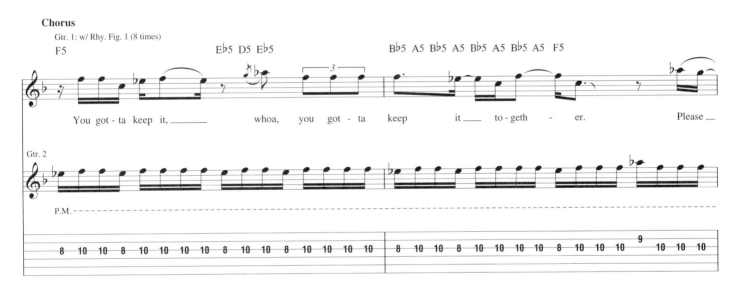

You got-ta keep it, _____ whoa, you got-ta keep it _____ to-geth - er. Please _____

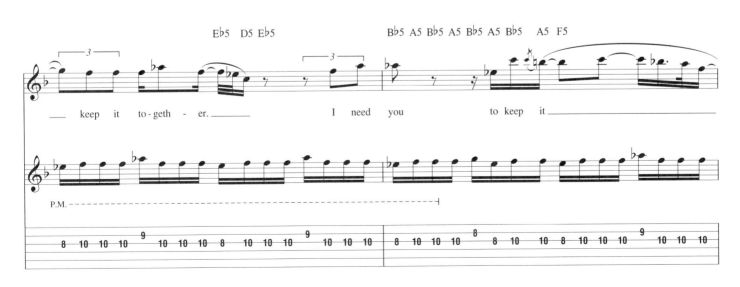

_____ keep it to-geth - er. _____ I need you to keep it _____

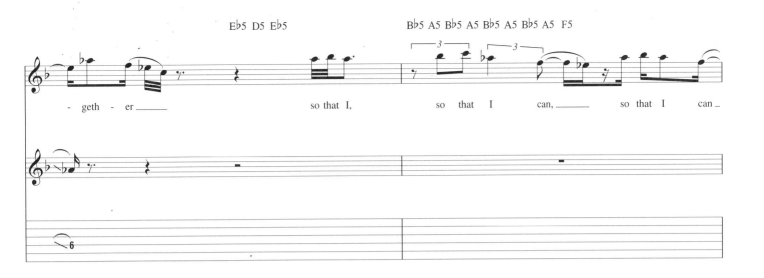

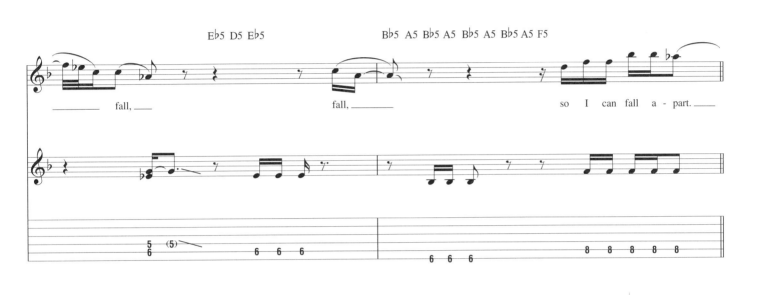

Outro

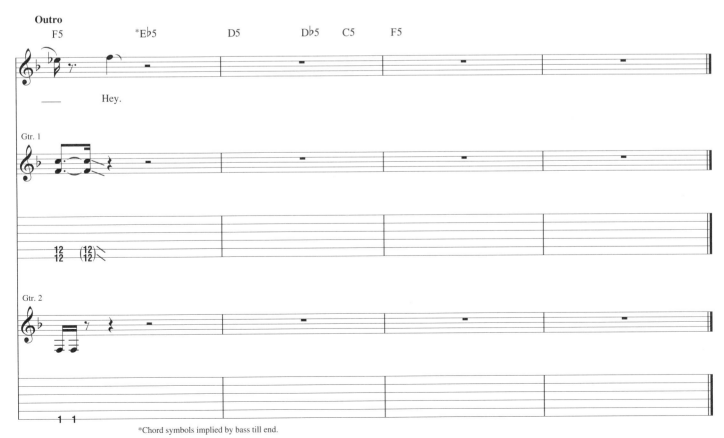

*Chord symbols implied by bass till end.

Boots Like These

Words and Music by Ben Harper, Jason Mozersky, Jordan Richardson and Jesse Ingalls

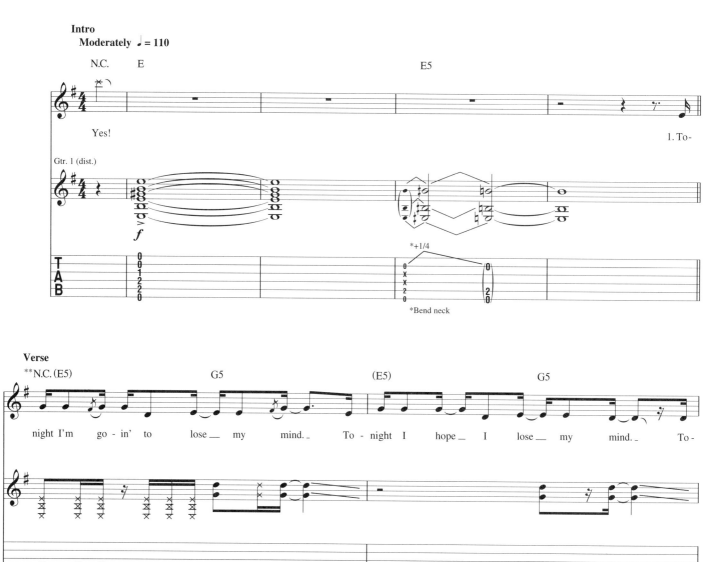

Verse

night we're gon - na live _ for - ev - er.   To - night _ we're gon - na live   for - ev - er.

N.C.

Nev - er pre - tend _____ to be a gam - bler. _____
(Whew!)

Interlude
E5

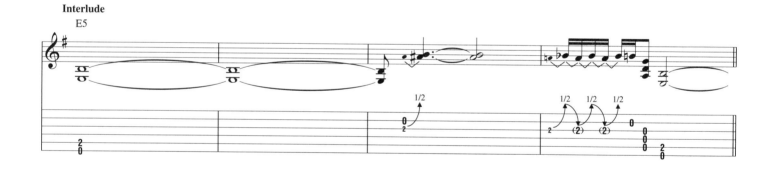

Verse
E5

3. The smoke from your lips, _   fire from _ your hips. _   She's just a slow walk - in' _____

*Sung behind the beat.

get out from ___ in - side ___ my head. Got - ta get out from in - side ___ my head. Got - ta

*w/ wah-wah

*+ = closed (toe down); ○ = open (toe up)

get out from ___ in - side ___ my head. _____ Dou - ble the dose ___ and I ran out - ta rope. It's me ___

___ and you a - gainst the world. ___ You dou - ble the dose ___ and I ran out - ta rope. It's me ___

___ and you a - gainst the world. ___

Gtr. 2 (dist.)

Gtr. 1

Guitar Solo

*Randomly rock wah-wah.

**w/ delay

let ring

**Set for 1 1/4 beats regeneration w/ 2 repeats.

wah-wah off

5. You got - ta

The Word Suicide

Words and Music by Ben Harper, Jason Mozersky, Jordan Richardson and Jesse Ingalls

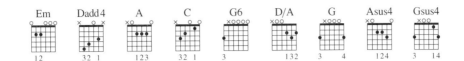

fered ____ to buy ___ me a ___ gun. What's so _____ hard a - bout ____

____ sym - pa - thy? ____ Love is a lone - ly ___ room. _____

Love is a lone - ly ___ room.

2. When

End Rhy. Fig. 1A

End Rhy. Fig. 1

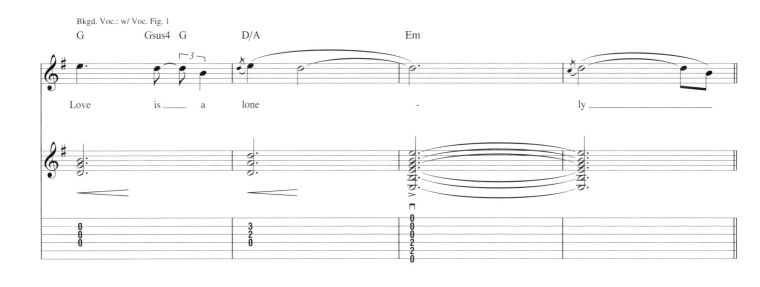

Guitar Solo

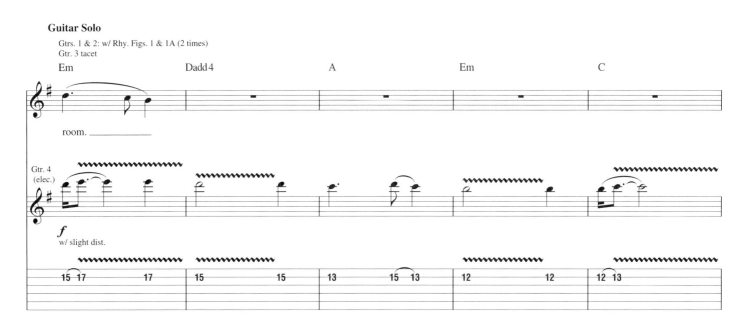

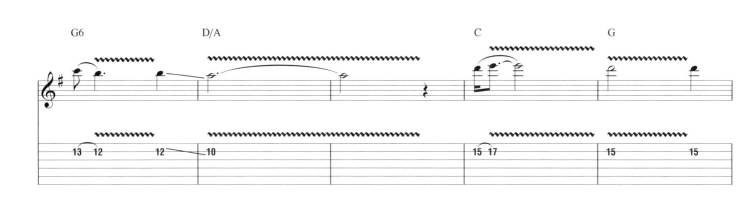

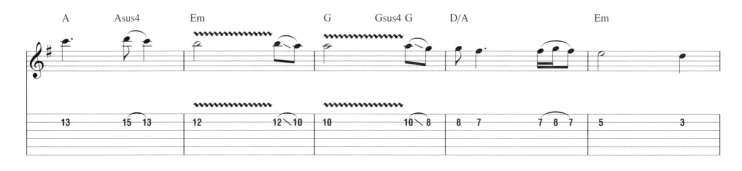

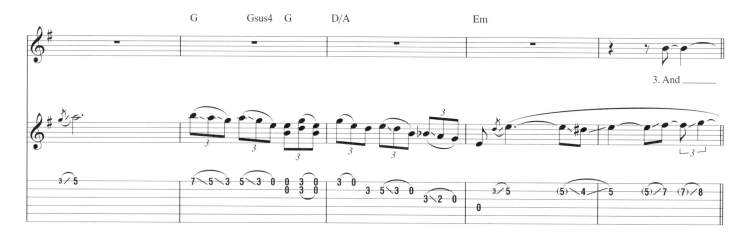

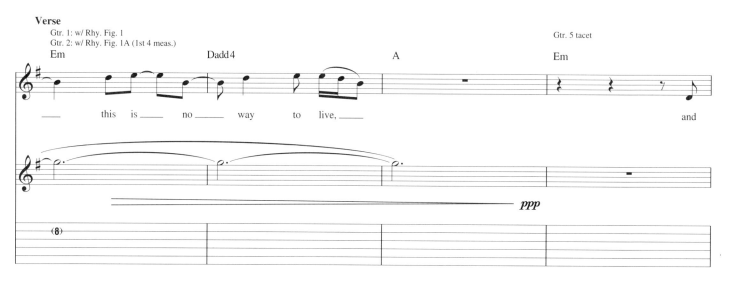

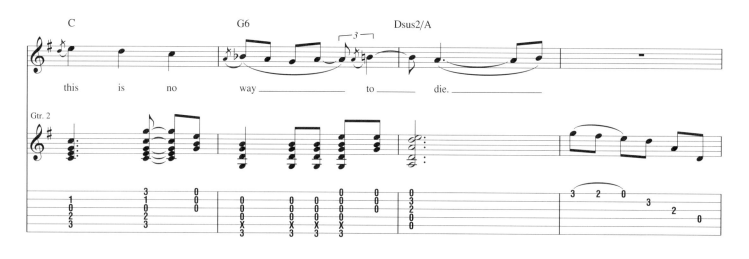

116

*Vol. swell   **Played behind the beat.

***Played as even eighth-notes.

119

Faithfully Remain

Words and Music by Ben Harper, Jason Mozersky, Jordan Richardson and Jesse Ingalls

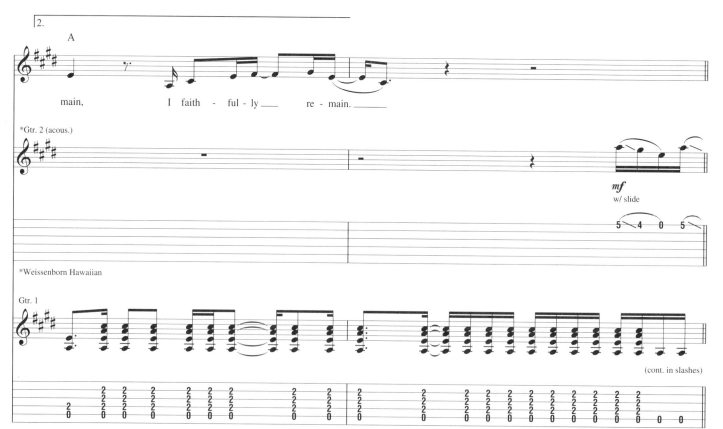

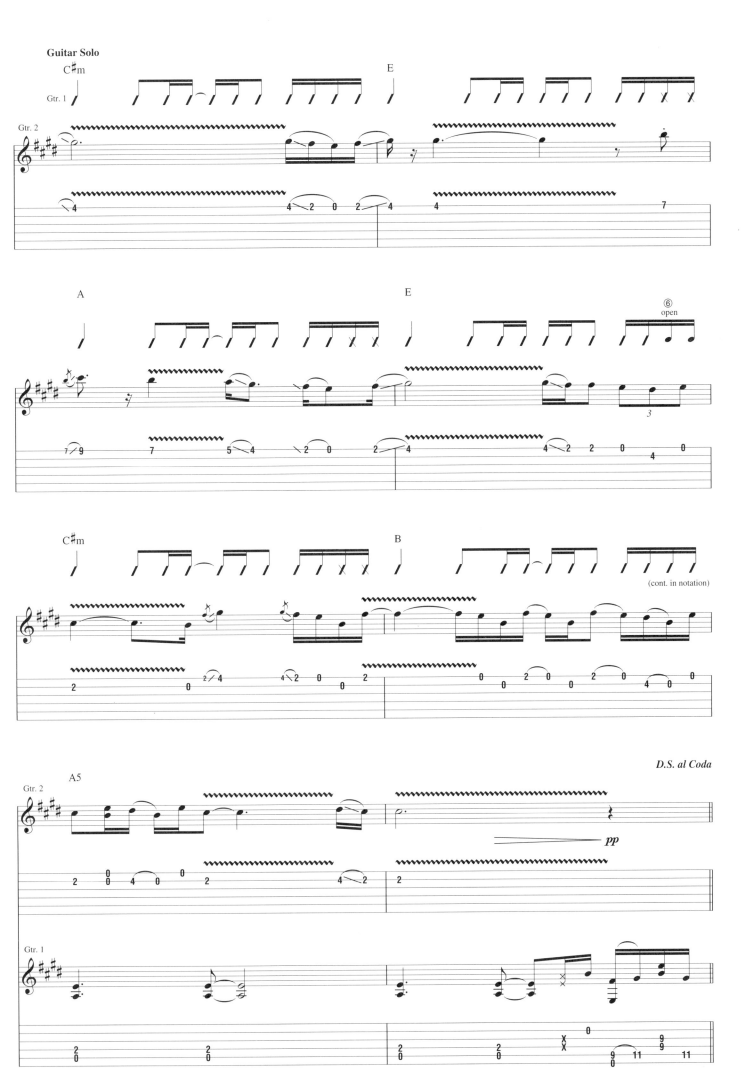

Coda

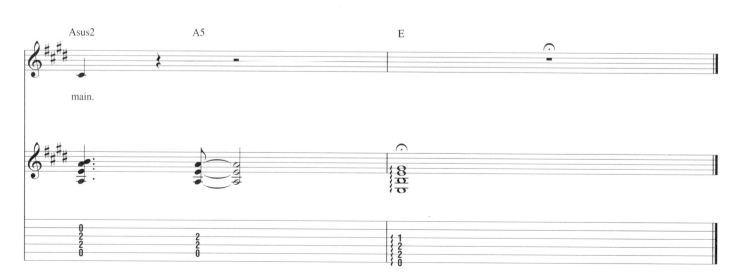

Guitar Notation Legend

Guitar music can be notated three different ways: on a *musical staff*, in *tablature*, and in *rhythm slashes*.

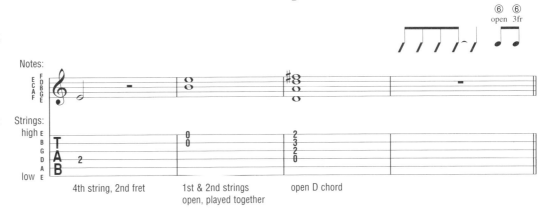

RHYTHM SLASHES are written above the staff. Strum chords in the rhythm indicated. Use the chord diagrams found at the top of the first page of the transcription for the appropriate chord voicings. Round noteheads indicate single notes.

THE MUSICAL STAFF shows pitches and rhythms and is divided by bar lines into measures. Pitches are named after the first seven letters of the alphabet.

TABLATURE graphically represents the guitar fingerboard. Each horizontal line represents a string, and each number represents a fret.

4th string, 2nd fret

1st & 2nd strings open, played together

open D chord

Definitions for Special Guitar Notation

HALF-STEP BEND: Strike the note and bend up 1/2 step.

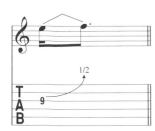

BEND AND RELEASE: Strike the note and bend up as indicated, then release back to the original note. Only the first note is struck.

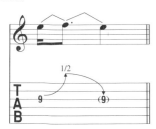

VIBRATO: The string is vibrated by rapidly bending and releasing the note with the fretting hand.

LEGATO SLIDE: Strike the first note and then slide the same fret-hand finger up or down to the second note. The second note is not struck.

WHOLE-STEP BEND: Strike the note and bend up one step.

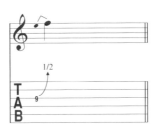

PRE-BEND: Bend the note as indicated, then strike it.

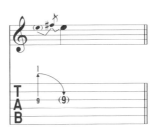

WIDE VIBRATO: The pitch is varied to a greater degree by vibrating with the fretting hand.

SHIFT SLIDE: Same as legato slide, except the second note is struck.

GRACE NOTE BEND: Strike the note and immediately bend up as indicated.

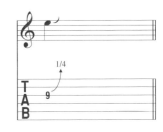

PRE-BEND AND RELEASE: Bend the note as indicated. Strike it and release the bend back to the original note.

HAMMER-ON: Strike the first (lower) note with one finger, then sound the higher note (on the same string) with another finger by fretting it without picking.

TRILL: Very rapidly alternate between the notes indicated by continuously hammering on and pulling off.

SLIGHT (MICROTONE) BEND: Strike the note and bend up 1/4 step.

UNISON BEND: Strike the two notes simultaneously and bend the lower note up to the pitch of the higher.

PULL-OFF: Place both fingers on the notes to be sounded. Strike the first note and without picking, pull the finger off to sound the second (lower) note.

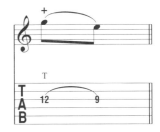

TAPPING: Hammer ("tap") the fret indicated with the pick-hand index or middle finger and pull off to the note fretted by the fret hand.

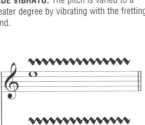

NATURAL HARMONIC: Strike the note while the fret-hand lightly touches the string directly over the fret indicated.

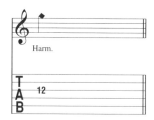

PINCH HARMONIC: The note is fretted normally and a harmonic is produced by adding the edge of the thumb or the tip of the index finger of the pick hand to the normal pick attack.

HARP HARMONIC: The note is fretted normally and a harmonic is produced by gently resting the pick hand's index finger directly above the indicated fret (in parentheses) while the pick hand's thumb or pick assists by plucking the appropriate string.

PICK SCRAPE: The edge of the pick is rubbed down (or up) the string, producing a scratchy sound.

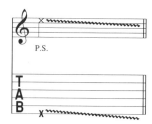

MUFFLED STRINGS: A percussive sound is produced by laying the fret hand across the string(s) without depressing, and striking them with the pick hand.

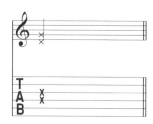

PALM MUTING: The note is partially muted by the pick hand lightly touching the string(s) just before the bridge.

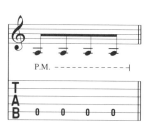

RAKE: Drag the pick across the strings indicated with a single motion.

TREMOLO PICKING: The note is picked as rapidly and continuously as possible.

ARPEGGIATE: Play the notes of the chord indicated by quickly rolling them from bottom to top.

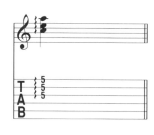

VIBRATO BAR DIVE AND RETURN: The pitch of the note or chord is dropped a specified number of steps (in rhythm), then returned to the original pitch.

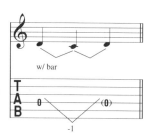

VIBRATO BAR SCOOP: Depress the bar just before striking the note, then quickly release the bar.

VIBRATO BAR DIP: Strike the note and then immediately drop a specified number of steps, then release back to the original pitch.

Additional Musical Definitions

(accent) • Accentuate note (play it louder).

(accent) • Accentuate note with great intensity.

(staccato) • Play the note short.

⊓ • Downstroke

V • Upstroke

D.S. al Coda • Go back to the sign (𝄋), then play until the measure marked "*To Coda*," then skip to the section labelled "**Coda**."

D.C. al Fine • Go back to the beginning of the song and play until the measure marked "*Fine*" (end).

Rhy. Fig. • Label used to recall a recurring accompaniment pattern (usually chordal).

Riff • Label used to recall composed, melodic lines (usually single notes) which recur.

Fill • Label used to identify a brief melodic figure which is to be inserted into the arrangement.

Rhy. Fill • A chordal version of a Fill.

tacet • Instrument is silent (drops out).

• Repeat measures between signs.

• When a repeated section has different endings, play the first ending only the first time and the second ending only the second time.

NOTE: Tablature numbers in parentheses mean:
1. The note is being sustained over a system (note in standard notation is tied), or
2. The note is sustained, but a new articulation (such as a hammer-on, pull-off, slide or vibrato) begins, or
3. The note is a barely audible "ghost" note (note in standard notation is also in parentheses).